THE HITTITES

THE STORY OF A FORGOTTEN EMPIRE

SLABS WITH HITTITE SCULPTURE.

THE HITTITES

THE STORY OF A FORGOTTEN EMPIRE

BY

A. H. SAYCE, LL.D., D.D.

LATE PROFESSOR OF ASSYRIOLOGY, OXFORD

AUTHOR OF

"FRESH LIGHT FROM THE ANCIENT MONUMENTS"
"ASSYRIA, ITS PRINCES, PRIESTS, AND PEOPLE," ETC., ETC.

REVISED AND ENLARGED EDITION

WITH TWELVE ILLUSTRATIONS

LONDON

THE RELIGIOUS TRACT SOCIETY

4 BOUVERIE STREET AND 65 ST. PAUL'S CHURCHYARD, E.C.

1925

First Edition published	-	1888
Second Edition ,,	-	1892
Third Edition ,,	-	1903
Fourth Edition ,,	-	1925

MADE IN GREAT BRITAIN
PRINTED BY THE WHITEFRIARS PRESS, LTD., LONDON AND TONBRIDGE

PREFACE TO THE THIRD EDITION

SINCE the first edition of this book was published fourteen years ago, " Hittitology," as our German friends call it, has become a recognized science. Hittite sites have been explored, fresh inscriptions been discovered, and a " Hittite " literature has grown up. M. Ménant, indeed, the learned translator of this volume into French, and one of the most devoted of Oriental students, has passed away, but his place has been supplied by young recruits of many nationalities. Various attempts have been made to decipher the inscriptions, among others by myself, but until the last few months the solution of the problem seemed as far off as ever.

I have at last succeeded, however, in partially lifting the veil which has hitherto concealed their meaning, and in the chapter relating to them will be found a brief outline of the process and its results. Before any system of decipherment can be accepted, there are three conditions which it has to fulfil. The right geographical names must be read without forcing in the inscriptions in which they would be expected to occur ; the grammar of the language must resemble that of the cuneiform tablets of Boghaz Keui and the Arzawan letters ; and the values assigned to the characters must support and corroborate one another. If the value is correct it will give us the name or grammatical form we want in each fresh text that we examine.

It is because all three conditions are fulfilled in the system of decipherment of which I here give a summary that its main conclusions may be accepted with confidence. Doubtless it is only a beginning, but in some cases " the beginning is half the whole." Our materials are still miserably imperfect : they often fail us where we most need them ; and inscriptions scattered over a wide area and of different dates are necessarily of less assistance to the decipherer than a group that comes from a single locality. What we want are more and better-preserved texts, above all, the systematic excavation of old Hittite sites like Boghaz Keui or Tyana, where we know that the archæological and epigraphic wealth is large. There is still much to be discovered even above ground. Two years ago

Mr. Anderson found a new text at Karaburna, in the valley of the Halys, and this year Dr. Belck has returned from his exploration of Kappadokia with a goodly spoil. Let us hope that before a new edition of this volume is called for, Dr. Leopold Messerschmidt's *Corpus inscriptionum Hettiticarum* may be doubled in size and the inscriptions within it fully explained.

A. H. SAYCE.

DAHABIA ISTAR, ASSIOUT.
December, 1902.

TABLE OF CONTENTS

LIST OF ILLUSTRATIONS

MAP ILLUSTRATING THE EXTENT OF THE HITTITE EMPIRE.

(Copied by permission from " The Empire of the Hittites.")

THE HITTITES

THE STORY OF A FORGOTTEN EMPIRE

CHAPTER I

THE HITTITES OF THE BIBLE

WE are told in the Second Book of Kings (vii. 6) that when the Syrians were encamped about Samaria and the Lord had sent a panic upon them, " they said one to another, Lo, the king of Israel hath hired against us the kings of the Hittites, and the kings of the Egyptians, to come upon us." About the year 1843 a distinguished scholar selected this passage for his criticism. Its " unhistorical tone," he declared, " is too manifest to allow of our easy belief in it." " No Hittite kings can have compared in power with the king of Judah, the real and near ally, who is not named at all . . . nor is there a single mark of acquaintance with the contemporaneous history."

Recent discoveries have retorted the critic's objections upon himself. It is not the Biblical writer but the modern author who is now proved to have been unacquainted with the contemporaneous history of the time. The Hittites were a very real power. Not very many centuries before the age of Elisha they had contested the empire of Western Asia with the Egyptians, and though their power had waned in the days of Jehoram they were still formidable enemies and useful allies. They were still worthy of comparison with the divided kingdom of Egypt, and infinitely more powerful than that of Judah.

But we hear no more about them in the subsequent records of the Old Testament. The age of Hittite supremacy belongs to an earlier date than the rise of the monarchy in Israel ; earlier, we may even say, than the Israelitish conquest of Canaan. The references to them in the later historical books of the Old Testament Canon are rare and scanty. The traitor who handed over Beth-el to the house of Joseph fled " into the land of the Hittites ' (Judges i. 26), and there built a city which he called Luz. Mr. Tomkins thinks he has found it in the town of Latsa, captured by the Egyptian king Ramses II, which he identifies with Qalb Luzeh in Northern Syria. However this may be, an emended reading of the text, based upon the Septuagint, transforms the unintelligible Tahtim-hodshi of 2 Sam. xxiv. 6 into " the Hittites of Kadesh," a city which long continued to be their chief stronghold in the valley of the Orontes. It was as far as this city, which lay at " the entering in of Hamath," on the northern frontier of the Israelitish kingdom, that the officers of David made their way when they were sent to number Israel. Lastly, in the reign of Solomon the Hittites are again mentioned (1 Kings x. 28, 29) in a passage where the authorized translation has obscured the sense. It runs in the Revised Version : " And the horses which Solomon had were brought out of Egypt ; and the king's merchants received them in droves, each drove at a price. And a chariot came up and went out of Egypt for six hundred shekels of silver, and an horse for an hundred and fifty : and so for all the kings of the Hittites, and for the kings of Syria, did they bring them out by their means." The Hebrew merchants, in fact, were the mediatories between Egypt and the north, and exported the horses of Egypt not only for the king of Israel but for the kings of the Hittites as well.

The Hittites whose cities and princes are thus referred to in the later historical books of the Old Testament belonged to the north, Hamath and Kadesh on the Orontes being their most southernly points. But the Book of Genesis introduces us to other Hittites—" the children of Heth," as they are termed—whose seats were in the extreme south of Palestine. It was from " Ephron the Hittite " that Abraham bought the cave of Machpelah at Hebron (Gen. xxiii.), and Esau " took to wife Judith the daughter of Beeri the Hittite, and Bashemath the daughter of Elon the Hittite " (Gen. xxvi. 34), or, as it is given elsewhere, " Adah the daughter of Elon the Hittite " (Gen. xxxvi. 2). It must be to these Hittites of the south that the ethnographical table in the tenth chapter of Genesis refers when it is said that " Canaan begat Sidon his firstborn, and Heth " (ver. 15), and in no other way can we explain the statement of Ezekiel (xvi. 3, 45) that " the father " of Jerusalem " was an Amorite and " its " mother a Hittite." " Uriah the Hittite," too, the trusty officer of David, must have come from the neighbourhood of Hebron, where David had reigned for seven years, rather than from among the distant Hittites of the north. Besides the latter there was thus a Hittite popula-

tion which clustered round Hebron, and to whom
the origin of Jerusalem was partly due.

Now it will be noticed that the prophet ascribes
the foundation of Jerusalem to the Amorite as well
as the Hittite. The Jebusites, accordingly, from
whose hands the city was wrested by David, must
have belonged to one or other of these two great
races ; perhaps, indeed, to both. At all events,
we find elsewhere that the Hittites and Amorites
are closely interlocked together. It was so at
Hebron, where in the time of Abraham not only
Ephron the Hittite dwelt, but also the three sons
of the Amorite Mamre (Gen. xiv. 13). The
Egyptian monuments show that the two nations
were similarly confederated together at Kadesh
on the Orontes. Kadesh was a Hittite stronghold ;
nevertheless it is described as being " in the land
of the Amaur " or Amorites, and its king is
depicted with the physical characteristics of the
Amorite, and not of the Hittite. Further north,
in the country which the Hittites had made
peculiarly their own, cities existed which belonged
to the Amorites, though they were built, as the
Hebrew writer expressed it, " in the land of
Canaan." Thus Shechem was taken by Jacob
" out of the hand of the Amorite " (Gen. xlviii. 22),

and the Amorite kingdom of Og and Sihon included large tracts on the eastern side of the Jordan. South of Palestine the block of mountains in which the sanctuary of Kadesh-barnea stood was an Amorite possession (Gen. xiv. 7, Deut. i. 19, 20) ; and we learn from Num. xiii. 29, that while the Amalekites dwelt " in the land of the south " and the Canaanites by the sea and in the valley of the Jordan, the Hittites and Jebusites and Amorites lived together in the mountains of the interior. Among the five kings of the Amorites against whom Joshua fought (Josh. x. 5) were the king of Jerusalem and the king of Hebron.

The Hittites and Amorites were therefore mingled together in the mountains of Palestine like the two races which ethnologists tell us go to form the modern Kelt. But the Egyptian monuments teach us that they were of very different origin and character. The Hittites were a people with yellow skins and " Mongoloid " features, whose receding foreheads, oblique eyes, and protruding upper jaws are represented as faithfully on their own monuments as they are on those of Egypt, so that we cannot accuse the Egyptian artists of caricaturing their enemies. If the Egyptians have made the Hittites ugly, it was because they were so in reality. The Amorites, on the contrary, were a tall and handsome people. They are depicted with white skins, blue eyes, and reddish hair, all the characteristics, in fact, of the white race. Prof. Petrie points out their resemblance to the Dardanians of Asia Minor, who form an intermediate link between the white-skinned tribes of the Greek seas and the fair-complexioned Libyans of Northern Africa. The latter are still found in large numbers in the mountainous regions which stretch eastward from Morocco, and are usually known among the French under the name of Kabyles. The traveller who first meets with them in Algeria cannot fail to be struck by their likeness to a certain part of the population in the British Isles. Their clear-white freckled skins, their blue eyes, their golden-red hair and tall stature, remind him of the fair Kelts of an Irish village ; and when we find that their skulls, which are of the so-called dolichocephalic or " long-headed " type, are the same as the skulls discovered in the prehistoric cromlechs of the country they still inhabit, we may conclude that they represent the modern descendants of the white-skinned Libyans of the Egyptian monuments.

In Palestine also we still come across representatives of a fair-complexioned blue-eyed race, in whom we may see the descendants of the ancient Amorites, just as we see in the Kabyles the descendants of the ancient Libyans. We know that the Amorite type continued to exist in Judah long after the Israelitish conquest of Canaan. The captives taken from the southern cities of Judah by Shishak in the time of Rehoboam, and depicted by him upon the walls of the great temple of Karnak are people of Amorite origin. Their " regular profile of sub-aquiline cast," as Mr. Tomkins describes it, their high cheek-bones and martial expression, are the features of the Amorites, and not of the Jews.

Tallness of stature has always been a distinguishing characteristic of the white race. Hence it was that the Anakim, the Amorite inhabitants of Hebron, seemed to the Hebrew spies to be as giants, while they themselves were but " as grasshoppers " by the side of them (Num. xiii. 33). After the Israelitish invasion remnants of the Anakim were left in Gaza and Gath and Ashkelon (Josh. xi. 22), and in the time of David Goliath of Gath and his gigantic family were objects of dread to their neighbours (2 Sam. xxi. 15–22).

It is clear, then, that the Amorites of Caanan belonged to the same white race as the Libyans of Northern Africa, and like them preferred the mountains to the hot plains and valleys below. The Libyans themselves belonged to a race which can be traced through the peninsula of Spain and the western side of France into the British Isles. Now it is curious that wherever this particular branch of the white race has extended it has been accompanied by a particular form of cromlech, or sepulchral chamber built of large uncut stones. The stones are placed upright in the ground and covered over with other large slabs, the whole chamber being subsequently concealed under a tumulus of small stones or earth. Not unfrequently the entrance to the cromlech is approached by a sort of corridor. These cromlechs are found in Britain, in France, in Spain, in Northern Africa, and in Palestine, more especially on the eastern side of the Jordan, and the skulls that have been exhumed from them are skulls of men of the dolichocephalic or long-headed type.

It has been necessary to enter at this length into what has been discovered concerning the Amorites by recent research, in order to show how carefully they should be to distinguish from the Hittites with whom they afterwards intermingled. They must have been in possession of Palestine long before the Hittites arrived there. They extended over a much wider area, since there are no traces of the Hittites at Shechem or on the eastern side of the Jordan, where the Amorites established two powerful kingdoms ; while the earliest mention of the Amorites in the Bible (Gen. xiv. 7) describes them as dwelling at Hazezon-tamar, or En-gedi, on the shores of the Dead Sea, where no Hittites are ever known to have settled. The Hittite colony in Palestine, moreover, was confined to a small district in the mountains of Judah : their strength lay far away in the north, where the Amorites were comparatively weak. It is true that Kadesh on the Orontes was in the hands of the Hittites ; but it is also true that it was " in the land of the Amorites," and this implies that they were its original occupants. We must regard the Amorites as the earlier population, among a part of whom the Hittites in later days settled and intermarried. At what epoch that event first took place we are still unable to say.

CHAPTER II

THE HITTITES ON THE MONUMENTS OF EGYPT AND ASSYRIA

IN the preceding chapter we have seen what the Bible has to tell us about " the children of Heth." They were an important people in the north of Syria who were ruled by " kings " in the days of Solomon, and whose power was formidable to their Syrian neighbours. But there was also a branch of them established in the extreme south of Palestine, where they inhabited the mountains along with the Amorites, and had taken a share in the foundation of Jerusalem. It was from one of the latter, Ephron the son of Zohar, that Abraham had purchased the cave of Machpelah at Hebron ; and one of the wives of Esau was of Hittite descent. In later times Uriah the Hittite was one of the chief officers of David, and his wife Bath-sheba was not only the mother of Solomon, but also the distant ancestress of Christ. For us, therefore, these Hittites of Judæa have a very special and peculiar interest.

The decipherment of the inscriptions of Egypt and Assyria has thrown a new light upon their origin and history, and shown that the race to which they belonged once played a leading part in the history of the civilized East. On the Egyptian monuments they are called Kheta (or better Khata), on those of Assyria Kkattâ or Khate, both words being exact equivalents of the Hebrew Kheth and Khitti.

The Kheta or Hittites first appear upon the scene in the time of the Eighteenth Egyptian Dynasty. The foreign rule of the Hyksos or Shepherd princes had been overthrown, Egypt had recovered its independence, and its kings determined to retaliate upon Asia the sufferings brought upon their own country by the Asiatic invader. The war, which commenced with driving the Asiatic out of the Delta, ended by attacking him in his own lands of Palestine and Syria. Thothmes I (about B.C. 1550) marched to the banks of the Euphrates and set up " the boundary of the empire " in the country of Naharina. Naharina was the Biblical Aram Naharaim or " Syria of the two rivers," better known, perhaps, as Mesopotamia, and its situation has been ascertained by recent discoveries. It was the district called Mitanni by the Assyrians,

who describe it as being " in front of the land of
the Hittites," on the eastern bank of the Euphrates,
between Carchemish and the mouth of the river
Balikh.   In the age of Thothmes I, it was the
leading state in Western Asia.   The Hittites had
not as yet made themselves formidable, and the
most dangerous enemy the Egyptian monarch was
called upon to face were the people over whom
Chushan-rishathaim   was   king   in   later   days
(Judges iii. 8).   It is not until the reign of his
grandson, Thothmes III, that the Hittites come
to the front.   Twice, he tells us, in B.C. 1470 and
1463, he received tribute from the king of the
land of the Hittites, " the Greater," which must
have been so called to distinguish it from a lesser
land of the Hittites elsewhere.   On the first
occasion the tribute consisted of eight rings of
silver 400 lbs. in weight, besides a " great piece of
crystal " and logs of hard wood.   On the second
occasion a considerable quantity of gold was sent
him as well as male and female negro-slaves, who
testify to a well-established trade between Asia
Minor and the Sudân.   Carchemish had already
fallen into the hands of the Egyptians, the city
having been stormed from the river-side ; though
whether it had been already wrested from its

Aramæan founders by the Hittites we do not know. Kadesh on the Orontes, at any rate, was not as yet a Hittite possession.

Before Thothmes died, he had made Egypt mistress of Palestine and Syria as far as the banks of the Euphrates and the land of Naharina. One of the bravest of his captains tells us on the walls of his tomb how he had captured prisoners in the neighbourhood of Aleppo, and had waded through the waters of the Euphrates when his master assaulted the mighty northern fortress of Carchemish. Kadesh on the Orontes had already fallen, and for a time all Western Asia did homage to the Egyptian monarch, even the king of Assyria sending him presents and courting, as it would seem, his allegiance. The Egyptian empire touched the land of Naharina on the east and the " greater land of the Hittites " on the north.

But neighbours so powerful could not remain long at peace. A fragmentary inscription records that the first campaign of Thothmes IV, the grandson of Thothmes III, was directed against the Hittites, and Amenophis III, the son and successor of Thothmes IV, found it necessary to support himself by entering into matrimonial alliance with the king of Naharina. The marriage had strange consequences for Egypt. The new queen brought with her not only a foreign name and foreign customs, but a foreign faith as well. She refused to worship Amon of Thebes and the other gods of Egypt, and clung to the religion of her fathers, whose supreme object of adoration was the solar disk. The Hittite monuments themselves bear witness to the prevalence of this worship in Northern Syria. The winged solar disk appears above the figure of a king which has been brought from Birejik on the Euphrates to the British Museum ; and even at Boghaz Keui, far away in Northern Asia Minor, the winged solar disk has been carved by Hittite sculptors upon the rock.

Amenophis IV, the son of Amenophis III, was educated in the faith of his mother, and after his accession to the throne endeavoured to impose the new creed upon his unwilling subjects. The powerful priesthood of Thebes withstood him for a while, but at last he assumed the name of Khu-n-Aten, " the refulgence of the solar disk," and quitting Thebes and its ancient temples he built himself a new capital dedicated to the new divinity. It stood on the eastern bank of the Nile, to the north of Assiout, and its long line of ruins is now known to the natives under the name of Tel el-

Amarna. The city was filled with the adherents of the new creed, and their tombs are yet to be found in the cliffs that enclose the desert on the east. Its existence, however, was of no long duration. After the death of Khu-n-Aten, " the heretic king," his throne was occupied by one or two princes who had embraced his faith ; but their reigns were brief, and they were succeeded by a monarch who returned once more to the religion of his forefathers. The capital of Khu-n-Aten was deserted, and the objects found upon its site show that it was never again inhabited.

Among its ruins a discovery has been made which casts an unexpected light upon the history of the Oriental world in the century before the Exodus. A large collection of clay tablets has been found, similar to those disinterred from the mounds of Nineveh and Babylonia, and like the latter inscribed in cuneiform characters and for the most part in the Assyro-Babylonian language. They consist almost wholly of letters and despatches sent to Khu-n-Aten and his father, Amenophis III, by the governors and rulers of Palestine, Syria, Mesopotamia, and Babylonia, and they prove that at that time Babylonian was the international language, and the complicated cuneiform system of

writing the common means of intercourse, of the
educated world. Many of them were transferred
by Khu-n-Aten from the royal archives of Thebes
to his new city at Tel el-Amarna ; the rest were
received and stored up after the new city had been
built. We learn from them that the Hittites were
already pressing southward, and were causing
serious alarm to the governors and allies of the
Egyptian king. One of the tablets is a despatch
from Northern Syria, praying the Egyptian
monarch to send assistance against them as soon
as possible.

Among the tablets is a letter from the Hittite
king himself. It is written in the Babylonian
language and characters, like the rest of the
correspondence, and proves that the Hittites of
the north participated in that literary culture of
Babylonia which was spread throughout Asia
Minor. Among them, as among the other nations
of the West, the language and script of diplomacy
were the Babylonian. It may be that the knowledge of the cuneiform syllabary had been received
from the Assyrian colonists settled in the south and
east of Kappadokia, in the country called Muzri,
" the Marches," by the Assyrians, where the great
mound of Kara Eyuk, eastward of Kaisariyeh, with

its layers of burnt ashes and its library of cuneiform tablets, testifies to the existence of an important Assyrian community as early as about B.C. 2300.

The Hittite king calls himself in his letter Subbi-luliuma, the Sapa-lul of the Egyptian monuments, and he writes to congratulate Amon-hotep IV on his accession to the throne. At the same time he takes occasion to remind the Egyptian monarch of his father's generosity; whatever the Hittite king asked for had been granted by the Pharaoh, and he is therefore now anxious to know why the Pharaoh's son is not equally liberal. Certain images of gold, for instance, and pieces of lapis lazuli which had been promised him had never been received. Accordingly he sends the Pharaoh, as a present, several objects of silver, with the further assurance that " whatever, my brother, you desire, write for it, and I will send it to you "; and he expects in return the gold and other things of which he is in need.

But though " the great king of the Hittites " condescended to make use of the international language of diplomacy, it was otherwise with another Hittite prince whose home was in Asia Minor. This was Tarkhundaraus the king of Arzawa. He too wrote to the Pharaoh in cuneiform characters, but the language he employed was that of his own country. It was, in fact, the language of the Hittites, and as we can read the cuneiform script, it gives us a welcome insight into the grammar and vocabulary of Hittite speech. There is another letter in the Tel el-Amarna collection in the same dialect, which, as we shall see, is also represented in certain cuneiform tablets found at Boghaz Keui. Arzawa was Western Cilicia, and at one time was tributary to the Hittite empire.

The Tel el-Amarna correspondence enables us to trace the southern progress of the Hittites in the closing days of the Egyptian empire and their conquest of Northern Syria. One by one the Egyptian fortresses fell into their hands ; religious discord prevented the Egyptian court from sending help to the beleaguered cities, and the Hittite invaders found themselves at last in the heart of the land of the Amorites, on the northern frontier of the later Palestine.

The Hittite general was Aita-gama. Amma was first occupied by him with the assistance of his brother-general, Dasa, and as Amma is the Ammo of the Old Testament to which Balaam belonged (Num. xxii. 5), it would seem probable that it was at this time that Pethor and the neighbouring Carchemish became Hittite. When Tunip, north-west of Aleppo, one of the most important of the Syrian strongholds of Egypt, surrendered to the invader, and Aita-gama with Arzawaya, " the man of Arzawa," pressed on further south, Kadesh on the Orontes yielded to their arms, and though Aita-gama professed to be acting on behalf of the Pharaoh (who was still the nominal ally of the Hittite king), and even had the audacity to write to Amon-hotep to that effect, and to claim that the district he had conquered had belonged to his father, the city passed for ever out of the permanent possession of Egypt. Henceforth it was to be a seat of Hittite power and influence.

But the onward march of the Hittite forces did not stop here. Marauding bands under military adventurers made their way into Canaan, and there sold their services to the Pharaoh, or carved out principalities for themselves with the sword. Arzawaya himself passed over to the Egyptian government, and wrote letters protesting his allegiance to it, while his sons established themselves in the extreme south of Palestine in the vicinity of Hebron. There, as we learn from the despatches of the king of Jerusalem, they joined the enemies of the Egyptian king and seized a portion of his territory.

They probably formed part of that body of raiders called Khabiri or " Confederates " in the Tel el-Amarna correspondence, who eventually captured Jerusalem, where they became the Jebusites of Hebrew history. At any rate, they serve to explain the existence of Hittite settlers within the borders of the tribe of Judah.

Egypt was too weak to expel them. The " heresy " of Khu-n-Aten had brought trouble and disorder into Egypt, and his immediate successors seem to have been forced to retire from Syria. So far from being able to aid their allies, the Egyptian generals found themselves no match for the Hittite armies. Ramses I, the founder of the Nineteenth Dynasty, was compelled to conclude a treaty, defensive and offensive, with the Hittite king Sapalul, and thus to recognize that Hittite power was on an equality with that of Egypt.

From this time forward it becomes possible to speak of a Hittite empire. Kadesh was in Hittite hands, and the influence formerly enjoyed by Egypt in Palestine and Syria was now enjoyed by its rival. The rude mountaineers of the Taurus had descended into the fertile plains of the south interrupting the intercourse between Babylonia and Canaan, and imposing Hittite governors upon the country. They had, however, long since adopted the elements of Babylonian civilization, including the use of the Babylonian script, and the Babylonian language continued to be the language of diplomacy and education.

With Seti I, the son and successor of Ramses, the power of Egypt again revived. He drove the Beduin and other marauders across the frontiers of the desert and pushed the war into Syria itself. The cities of the Philistines again received Egyptian garrisons ; Seti marched his armies as far as the Orontes, fell suddenly upon Kadesh and took it by storm. The war was now begun between Egypt and the Hittites, which lasted for the next half-century. It left Egypt utterly exhausted, and, in spite of the vainglorious boasts of its scribes and poets, glad to make a peace which virtually handed over to her rivals the possession of Northern Syria.

But at first success waited on the arms of Seti. He led his armies once more to the Euphrates and the borders of Naharina, and compelled Mutal, the Hittite monarch, to sue for peace. The natives of the Lebanon received him with acclamations, and cut down their cedars for his ships on the Nile.

When Seti died, however, the Hittites were again in possession of Kadesh, and war had broken out between them and his son Ramses II. The long reign of Ramses II was a ceaseless struggle against his formidable foes. The war was waged with varying success. Sometimes victory inclined to the Egyptians, sometimes to their Hittite enemies. Its chief result was to bring ruin and disaster upon the cities of the Canaanites. Their land was devastated by the hostile armies which traversed it ; their towns were sacked, now by the Hittite invaders from the north, now by the soldiers of Ramses from the south. It was little wonder that their inhabitants fled to island fastnesses like Tyre, deserting the city on the mainland, which an Egyptian traveller of the age of Ramses tells us had been burnt not long before. We can understand now why they offered so slight a resistance to the invading Israelites. The Exodus took place shortly after the death of Ramses II, the Pharaoh of the oppression ; and when Joshua entered Palestine he found there a disunited people and a country exhausted by the long and terrible wars of the preceding century. The way had been prepared by the Hittites for the Israelitish conquest of Canaan.

Pentaur, a sort of Egyptian poet laureate, has left us an epic which records the heroic deeds of Ramses

in his first campaign against the Hittites. The
actual event which gave occasion to it was an act of
bravery performed by the Egyptian monarch before the walls of Kadesh ; but the poet has transformed him into a hero capable of superhuman
deeds, and has thus produced an epic poem which
reminds us of the Greek Iliad. Its details, however, afford a welcome insight into the history of
the time, and show to what a height of power the
Hittite empire had advanced. Its king could
summon to his aid vassal-allies not only from
Syria, but from the distant regions of Asia Minor
as well. The merchants of Carchemish, the
islanders of Arvad, acknowledged his supremacy
along with the Dardanians of the Troad and the
Lykians of Cilicia. The Hittite empire was already
a reality, extending from the banks of the Euphrates
to the shores of the Ægean, and including both
the cultured Semites of Syria and the rude bar-
barians of the Greek seas.

It was in the fifth year of the reign of Ramses
(B.C. 1283) that the event occurred which was
celebrated by the Egyptian Homer. The Egyptian
armies had advanced to the Orontes and the
neighbourhood of Kadesh. There two Beduin
spies were captured, who averred that the Hittite

king was far away in the north with his forces, encamped at Aleppo. But the intelligence was false. The Hittites and their allies, multitudinous as the sand on the sea-shore, were really lying in ambush hard by. In their train were the soldiers of Naharina, of the Dardanians and of Mysia, along with numberless other peoples who now owned the Hittite sway. The Hittite monarch " had left no people on his road without bringing them with him. Their number was endless ; nothing like it had ever been before. They covered mountains and valleys like grasshoppers for their number. He had not left silver or gold with his people ; he had taken away all their goods and possessions to give it to the people who accompanied him to the war."

The whole host was concealed in ambush on the north-west side of Kadesh. Suddenly they arose and fell upon the terrified Egyptians by the waters of the Lake of the Amorites, the modern Lake of Homs. The chariots and horses charged " the legion of Ra-Harmakhis," and " foot and horse gave way before them." The news was carried to the Pharaoh. " He arose like his father Mentu, he grasped his weapons, and put on his armour like Baal." His steed " Victory in Thebes " bore him in his chariot into the midst of the foe. Then he looked behind him, and behold he was alone. The bravest heroes of the Hittite host beset his retreat, and 2,500 hostile chariots were around him. He was abandoned in the midst of the enemy : not a prince, not a captain was with him. Then in his extreme need the Pharaoh called upon his god Amon. " Where art thou, my father Amon ? If this means that the father has forgotten his son, have I done anything without thy knowledge, or have I not gone and followed the precepts of thy mouth ? Never were the precepts of thy mouth transgressed, nor have I broken thy command- ments in any respect. Sovran lord of Egypt, who makest the peoples that withstand thee to bow down, what are these people of Asia to thy heart ? Amon brings them low who knows not God. . . . Behold now, Amon, I am in the midst of many unknown peoples in great number. All have united themselves, and I am all alone : no other is with me ; my warriors and my charioteers have deserted me. I called to them, and not one of them heard my voice."

The petition of Ramses was heard. Amon " reached out his hand," and declared that he was come to help the Pharaoh against his foes. Then

Ramses was inspired with supernatural strength. " I hurled," he is made to say, " the dart with my right hand, I fought with my left hand. I was like Baal in his hour before their sight. I had found 2,500 chariots ; I was in the midst of them ; but they were dashed in pieces before my horses." The ground was covered with the slain, and the Hittite king fled in terror. His princes again gathered round the Pharaoh, and again Ramses scattered them in a moment. Six times did he charge the Hittite host, and six times they broke and were slaughtered. The strength of Baal was " in all the limbs " of the Egyptian king.

Now at last his servants came to his aid. But the victory had already been won, and all that remained was for the Pharaoh to upbraid his army for their cowardice and sloth. " Have I not given what is good to each of you," he exclaims, " that ye have left me, so that I was alone in the midst of hostile hosts ? Forsaken by you my life was in peril, and you breathed tranquilly, and I was alone. Could you not have said in your hearts that I was a rampart of iron to you ? " It was the horses of the royal chariot and not the troops who deserved reward, and who would obtain it when the king arrived safely home. So Ramses " returned in victory and strength ; he had smitten hundreds of thousands all together in one place with his arm."

At daybreak the following morning he desired to renew the conflict. The serpent that glowed on the front of his diadem " spat fire " in the face of his enemies. They were overawed by the deeds of valour he had accomplished single-handed the day before, and feared to resume the fight. " They remained afar off, and threw themselves down on the earth, to entreat the king in the sight [of his army]. And the king had power over them and slew them without their being able to escape. As bodies tumbled before his horses, so they lay there stretched out all together in their blood. Then the king of the hostile people of the Hittites sent a messenger to pray piteously to the great name of the king, speaking thus : ' Thou art Ra-Harmakhis. Thy terror is upon the land of the Hittites, for thou hast broken the neck of the Hittites for ever and ever.' "

The army of Ramses seconded the prayer of the herald that the Egyptians and Hittites should henceforward be " brothers together." A treaty was accordingly made ; but it was soon broken, and it was not until sixteen years later that peace was finally established between the two rival powers.

The act of personal prowess upon which the heroic poem of Pentaur was built may have covered what had really been a check to the Egyptian arms. At all events, it is significant that no attempt was made to capture Kadesh, and that even the poet acknowledges how ready the Egyptian soldiers were to come to terms with their enemies. Equally significant is the fact that the war against the Hittites still went on ; in the eighth year of the Pharaoh's reign Palestine was overrun and certain cities captured, including Dapur or Tabor " in the land of the Amorites," while other campaigns were directed against Ashkelon, in the south, and the city of Tunip or Tennib, in the north. When a lasting treaty of peace was at last concluded in the twenty-first year of Ramses, its conditions show that " the great king of the Hittites " treated on equal terms with the great king of Egypt, and that even Ramses himself, whom later legend magnified into the Sesostris of the Greeks, was fain to acknowledge the power of his Hittite adversaries. The treaty was sealed by the marriage of the Pharaoh with the daughter of the Hittite king.

The treaty, of which we possess the Egyptian text in full, was a very remarkable one, not only because it is the first treaty of the kind of which we know, but also on account of its contents. It ran as follows [1] :—

" In the year twenty-one, in the month Tybi, on the 21st day of the month, in the reign of King Ramessu-Miamun, the dispenser of life eternally and for ever, the beloved of the divinities Amon-Ra (of Thebes), Harmakhu (of Heliopolis), Ptah (of Memphis), Mut the lady of the Asher-lake (near Karnak), and Khonsu, the peace-loving, being arisen upon the throne of Horus among the living, resembling his father Harmakhu in eternity, in eternity, evermore.

" On that day the king was in the city of Ramses, presenting his peace-offerings to his father Amon-Ra, and to the gods Harmakhu, Tum, Ptah of Ramessu-Miamun, and Sutekh, the strong, the son of the goddess of heaven Nut, that they might grant to him many thirty years' jubilee feasts, and innumerable happy years, and the subjection of all peoples under his feet for ever.

[1] This translation is the one given by Brugsch in the second edition of the English translation of his *History of Egypt*, with corrections from Dr. A. H. Gardiner's version, *Journal of Egyptian Archæology*, vi. 3 (1920).

" Then came forward the ambassador of the king, and the Adon [of his house, by name . . . and presented the ambassadors] of the great king of the Hittites, Khattu-sil, who were sent to Pharaoh to propose friendship with the king Ramessu-Miamun, the dispenser of life eternally and for ever, just as his father the Sun-god [dispenses it] each day.

" This is the copy of the contents of the silver tablet, which the great king of the Hittites, Khattu-sil, had caused to be made, and which was presented to the Pharaoh by the hand of his ambassador Tal-tesub and his ambassador Ra-mes, to propose friendship with the king Ramessu-Miamun, the bull among the princes, who places his boundary-marks where it pleases him in all lands.

" The treaty which had been proposed by the great king of the Hittites, Khattu-sil, the powerful, the son of Mur-sil, the powerful, the son of the son of Sapa-lul, the great king of the Hittites, the powerful, on the silver tablet, to Ramessu-Miamun, the great prince of Egypt, the powerful, the son of Meneptah Seti, the great prince of Egypt, the powerful, the son's son of Ramessu I, the great king of Egypt, the powerful—this was a good treaty for friendship and concord, which assured peace [and established concord] by means of [a treaty between the Hittites and Egypt] for ever. For it was the agreement of the great prince of Egypt in common with the great king of the Hittites, that the god should not allow enmity to exist between them, on the basis of a treaty.

" To wit, in the times of Mutal, the great king of the Hittites, my brother, he was at war with [Meneptah Seti] the great prince of Egypt.

" But now, from this very day forward, Khattusil, the great king of the Hittites, shall look upon this treaty, so that the policy may remain, which the god Ra has made, which the god Sutekh has provided, for the people of Egypt and for the people of the Hittites, that there should be no more enmity between them for evermore."

And these are the contents :—

" Khattu-sil, the great king of the Hittites, is in covenant with Ramessu-Miamun, the great prince of Egypt, from this very day forward, that there may subsist a good friendship and a good understanding between them for evermore.

" He shall be my ally ; he shall be my friend : I will be his ally ; I will be his friend : for ever.

" And since that Mutal, the great king of the

Hittites, my brother, hastened after his fate, and Khattu-sil placed himself on the throne of his father as the great king of the Hittites, I strive for friendship with Ramessu-Miamun, the great prince of Egypt, and it is [my wish] that the friendship and the concord may be better than the friendship and the concord which before existed in the land of the Hittites.

" I declare : I, the great king of the Hittites, will hold together with [Ramessu-Miamun], the great prince of Egypt, in good friendship and in good concord. The sons of the sons of the great king of the Hittites will hold together and be friends with the sons of the sons of Ramessu-Miamun, the great prince of Egypt.

" In virtue of our treaty for concord, and in virtue of our policy [for friendship, let the people] of Egypt [be united in friendship] with the people of the Hittites. Let a like friendship and a like concord subsist in such manner for ever.

" Never let enmity rise between them. Never let the great king of the Hittites invade the land of Egypt, if anything shall have been plundered from it. Never let Ramessu-Miamun, the great prince of Egypt, overstep the boundary of the land of the Hittites, to take any plunder from it.

" The regular treaty, which existed in the times of Sapa-lul, the great king of the Hittites, likewise the just treaty which existed in the times of Mutal, the great king of the Hittites, my brother, that will I keep.

" Ramessu-Miamun, the great prince of Egypt, declares that he will keep it. [We have come to an understanding about it] with one another at the same time from this day forward, and we will fulfil it, and will act in a righteous manner.

" If another shall come as an enemy to the lands of Ramessu-Miamun, the great prince of Egypt, then let him send an embassy to the great king of the Hittites to this effect : ' Come with me as help against him.' Then shall the great king of the Hittites [assemble his warriors], and the king of the Hittites [shall come] to smite his enemies. But if it should not be the wish of the great king of the Hittites to march out in person, then he shall send his warriors and his chariots, that they may smite his enemies. Or if Ramessu-Miamun [the great king of Egypt] is offended with any of his servants and they commit sin against him and he goes to smite his enemy, the great king of the Hittites shall combine with him [to destroy] every one [with whom] he is offended. The great king of the

Hittites shall act in common with [the great prince of Egypt.

" If another should come as an enemy to the lands of the great king of the Hittites, then shall he send an embassy to the great prince of Egypt with the request that] he would come in great power to kill his enemies ; and if it be the desire of Ramessu-Miamun, the great prince of Egypt, to come (himself), he shall [smite the enemies of the great king of the Hittites. If it is not the desire of the great prince of Egypt to march out in person, then he shall send his warriors and his two-] horse chariots, while he sends back the answer to the people of the Hittites.

" If any subjects of the great king of the Hittites have offended him, then Ramessu-Miamun, [the great prince of Egypt, shall not receive them in his land, but shall advance to kill them] . . . the oath, with the wish to say : I will go . . . until . . . Ramessu-Miamun, the great prince of Egypt, living for ever . . . that he may be given for them (?) to the lord, and that Ramessu-Miamun, the great prince of Egypt, may speak according to his agreement evermore. . . .

" [If servants shall flee away] out of the territories of Ramessu-Miamun, the great prince of Egypt, to betake themselves to the great king of the Hittites, the great king of the Hittites shall not receive them, but the great king of the Hittites shall give them up to Ramessu-Miamun, the great prince of Egypt, [that they may receive their punishment].

" If one or two men of the lower class flee [from Egypt], and betake themselves to the land of the Hittites, to make themselves servants of another, they shall not remain in the land of the Hittites ; [they shall be given up] to Ramessu-Miamun, the great prince of Egypt.

" Or if a man of the upper class flee from the land of the Hittites and betake himself to Ramessu-Miamun, the great prince of Egypt, [in order to stay in Egypt], then those who have come from the land of the Hittites in order to betake themselves to Ramessu-Miamun, the great prince of Egypt, shall not be [received by] Ramessu-Miamun, the great prince of Egypt, [but] the great prince of Egypt, Ramessu-Miamun, [shall deliver them up to the great king of the Hittites].

" If one or two men of the lower class flee [from the land of the Hittites], so that they come to the land of Egypt to make themselves servants of another, then Ramessu-Miamun will not allow them to settle, he will deliver them up to the great king of the Hittites.

" As for the words of this treaty [which has been drawn up between] the great king of the Hittites and Ramessu-Miamun, the great king [of Egypt, in] writing upon this tablet of silver—as for these words the thousand gods, male and female, among those of the gods of Egypt, they are witnesses with me [to the validity] of these words :—

(1) The Sun-god, the lord of heaven ;

(2) The Sun-god of the city of the land of Arinna (near Komana) ;

(3) Sutekh, the lord of heaven ;

(4) Sutekh of the land of the Hittites ;

(5) Sutekh of the city of the land of Arinna ;

(6) Sutekh of the city of the land of Zippa- landa ;

(7) Sutekh of the city of the land of Pe[tia]- rik ;

(8) Sutekh of the city of the land of Khisas- khapa ;

(9) Sutekh of the city of the land of Sarisu (the classical Sareisa) ;

(10) Sutekh of the city of the land of Khilpa (Aleppo) ;

(11) Sutekh of the city of the land of Rukha-
sina [1] ;

. . . .

(14) [Sutekh of the city of the land] of . . sa ;
(15) Sutekh of the city of the land of Sakhi-
paina ;
(16) Antharta (Astoreth) of the territory of the
land of the Hittites ;
(17) The god of the land of Zitkhirri ;
(18) The god of [the land] of Karz[is] ;
(19) The god of the land of Kharpantalis ;
(20) The goddess of the city of the [land of]
Karakhna ;

. . . .

(23) The goddess of the land of Khuakha (?) ;
(24) The goddess of the land of Zin[ath] ;
(25) The god of [the land of] Zi . . ta ;
(26) The god of the land of Sa . . rpa (?) ;
(27) The god of the land of Khibat, the queen
of heaven ;
(28) The divine lords of oaths ;
(29) The goddess mistress of the soil ;
(30) The mistress of the oath ;

[1] Called Rukhizzi in the Tel el-Amarna tablets. Arzawaya was its
prince.

(31) Askhir (Babylonian Iskhara), the goddess, mistress of the mountains ;

(32) The rivers of the land of the Hittites ;

(33) The gods of the land of Qizuwadna ;

(34) Amon-Ra, Sutekh and the male and female deities of the mountains and rivers of the land of Egypt, the sky, the soil, the great lakes, the winds and the storms.[1]

" With regard to these words which are upon the silver tablet of the people of the Hittites and of the people of Egypt, he who shall not observe them the thousand gods of the land of the Hittites and the thousand gods of the land of Egypt shall destroy his house, his land and his servants.

" But he who shall observe these words which the silver tablet contains, whether he be of the people of the Hittites or [of the people of Egypt], because he has not neglected them, the thousand gods of the land of the Hittites and the thousand gods of the land of Egypt shall secure his health and preserve life [for him] and his servants together with his houses, his [land] and his servants.

" If there flee away of the inhabitants [one from the land of Egypt], or two or three, and they betake

[1] The above list of deities and localities is from a corrected copy of the inscription made by myself.

themselves to the great king of the Hittites [the great king of the Hittites shall not] allow them [to remain, but he shall] deliver them up, and send them back to Ramessu-Miamun, the great prince of Egypt.

" Now with respect to the [inhabitant of the land of Egypt], who is delivered up to Ramessu-Miamun, the great prince of Egypt, his fault shall not be avenged upon him, his [house] shall not be taken away, nor his [wife] nor his [children]. Let him not be [put to death], neither let him be punished in his eyes, nor on his mouth, nor on the soles of his feet, so that thus no crime shall be brought forward against him.

" In the same way shall it be done if inhabitants of the land of the Hittites take to flight, be it one alone, or two, or three, to betake themselves to Ramessu-Miamun, the great prince of Egypt. Ramessu-Miamun, the great prince of Egypt, shall cause them to be seized, and they shall be delivered up to the great king of the Hittites.

" [With regard to] him who [is delivered up, his crime shall not be brought forward against him]. His [house] shall not be taken away, nor his wives, nor his children, nor his people ; he shall not be put to death nor be punished in his ears or his eyes, nor on his mouth, nor on the soles of his feet, nor shall any accusation be brought forward against him.

"That which is on the silver tablet, on the obverse represents Sutekh embracing the great king of the Hittites, surrounded by an inscription to this effect : ' The seal of Sutekh the prince of heaven,' being the seal of the treaty made by Khattu-sil, the son of Mur-sil, the great and powerful king of the Hittites. That which is in the middle of the engraved border is the seal of [Sutekh the prince of heaven]. That which is on the engraved reverse represents the image of [the goddess] of the Hittites embracing the great queen of the Hittites, surrounded by an inscription to this effect : ' The seal of the Sun-goddess of the city of Arinna, the lady of the land,' and ' The seal of Putu-khepa the great queen of the land of the Hittites, the daughter of the land of Qizu[wadna, the princess of the city] of the land of Arinna, the mistress of (its) territory, the priestess of the goddess.' That which is within the engraved border is the seal of the Sun-goddess of Arinna, the lady of the whole earth." [1]

---

[1] The last paragraph is translated from a copy of the text made by M. Bouriant and revised by myself.

This compact of offensive and defensive alliance proves more forcibly than any description the position to which the Hittite empire had attained. It ranked side by side with the Egypt of Ramses, the last great Pharaoh who ever ruled over the land of the Nile. With Egypt it had contested the sovereignty of Western Asia, and had compelled the Egyptian monarch to consent to peace. Egypt and the Hittites were now the two leading powers of the world.

The treaty was ratified by the visit of the Hittite prince Khattu-sil to Egypt in his national costume, and the marriage of his daughter to Ramses in the thirty-fourth year of the Pharaoh's reign (B.C. 1254). She took the Egyptian name of Ur-maa Noferu-Ra, and her beauty was celebrated by the scribes of the court. Syria was handed over to the Hittites as their legitimate possession ; Egypt never again attempted to wrest it from them, and if the Hittite yoke was to be shaken off it must be through the efforts of the Syrians themselves. For a while, however, " the great king of the Hittites " preserved his power intact ; his supremacy was acknowledged from the Euphrates in the east to the Ægean Sea in the west, from Kappadokia in the north to the tribes of Canaan in the south.

Even Naharina, once the antagonist of the Egyptian Pharaohs, acknowledged his sovereignty, and Pethor, the home of Balaam, at the junction of the Euphrates and the Sajur, became a Hittite town. The cities of Philistia, indeed, still sent tribute to the Egyptian ruler, but northwards the Hittite sway seems to have been omnipotent. The Amorites of the mountains allied themselves with " the children of Heth," and the Canaanites in the lowlands looked to them for protection. The Israelites had not as yet thrust themselves between the two great powers of the Oriental world : it was still possible for a Hittite sovereign to visit Egypt, and for an Egyptian traveller to explore the cities of Canaan.

After sixty-seven years of vainglorious splendour the long reign of Ramses II came to an end (B.C. 1221). The Israelites had toiled for him in building Pithom and Raamses, and on the accession of his son and successor, Meneptah, they demanded permission to depart from Egypt. The history of the Exodus is too well known to be recounted here ; it marks the close of the period of conquest and prosperity which Egypt had enjoyed under the kings of the eighteenth and nineteenth dynasties. Early in his reign Meneptah had sent corn by sea

to the Hittites at a time when there was a famine
in Syria, showing that the peaceful relations established during the reign of his father were still in
force. Despatches dated in his third year also
exist, which speak of letters and messengers passing
to and fro between Egypt and Phœnicia, and make
it clear that Gaza was still garrisoned by Egyptian
troops. But in the fifth year of his reign Egypt was
invaded by a confederacy of white-skinned tribes
from Libya and the shores of Asia Minor, who
overran the Delta and threatened the very existence
of the Egyptian monarchy. Egypt, however, was
saved by a battle in which the invading host was
almost annihilated, but not before it had itself
been half drained of its resources, and weakened
correspondingly.

Not many years afterwards the dynasty of
Ramses the Oppressor descended to its grave in
bloodshed and disaster. Civil war broke out, followed by foreign invasion, and the crown was
seized by " Arisu the Phœnician." But happier
times again arrived. Once more the Egyptians
obeyed a native prince, and the Twentieth Dynasty
was founded. Its one great king was Ramses III,
who rescued his country from two invasions more
formidable even than that which had been beaten

back by Meneptah. Like the latter, they were conducted by the Libyans and the nations of the Greek seas, and the invaders were defeated partly on the land, partly on the water. The maritime confederacy included the Danaans of Greece, the Lykians and the Philistines, perhaps also the natives of Sardinia and Sicily. They had flung themselves in the first instance on the coasts of Phœnicia, and spread inland as far as Carchemish. Laden with spoil, they fixed their camp " in the land of the Amorites," and then descended upon Egypt. The Hittites of Carchemish and the people of Mitanni or Naharina came in their train, and a long and terrible battle took place on the sea-shore in the neighbourhood of Egypt. The Egyptians were victorious ; the ships of the enemy were sunk, and their soldiers slain or captured. Egypt was once more filled with captives, and the flame of its former glory flickered again for a moment before finally going out.

The list of prisoners shows that the Hittite tribes had taken part in the struggle, Carchemish, Aleppo, and Pethor being named among the enemies of the Egyptian king. They had probably marched by land, while their allies from Asia Minor and the islands of the Mediterranean had attacked the

Egyptian coast in ships. So far as we can gather, the Hittite populations no longer acknowledged the suzerainty of an imperial sovereign, but were divided into independent states. It would seem, too, that they had lost their hold upon Mysia and the far west. The Zakkal and the Danaans, the Shardaina and the Shakalsha are said to have attacked their cities before proceeding on their southward march. If we can trust the statement, we must conclude that the Hittite empire had already broken up. The tribes of Asia Minor it had conquered were in revolt, and had carried the war into the homes of their former masters. Meshech, the Moschian, had taken the place of the Hittites of Boghaz Keui and a new empire, that of Cilicia, had been established. Little by little the Aramæan population pushed the Hittite back into his northern fastnesses, and throughout the period of the Israelitish judges we never hear even of his name. The Hittite chieftains advance no longer to the south of Kadesh ; and though Israel was once oppressed by a king who had come from the north, he was king of Aram-Naharaim, the Naharina of the Egyptian texts, and not a Hittite but a Moschian prince.

Where the Egyptian monuments desert us, those

of Assyria come to our help. The earliest notices of the Hittites found in the cuneiform texts are contained in a great work on astronomy and astrology, originally compiled for an early king of Babylonia. The references to " the king of the Hittites," however, which meet us in it, cannot be ascribed to a remote date. One of the chief objects aimed at by the author (or authors) of the work was to foretell the future, it being supposed that a particular event which had followed a certain celestial phenomenon would be repeated when the phenomenon happened again. Consequently it was the fashion to introduce into the work from time to time fresh notices of events ; and some of these glosses, as we may term them, are probably not older than the seventh century B.C. It is, therefore, impossible to determine the exact date to which the allusions to the Hittite king belong, but there are indications that it is comparatively late. The first clear account that the Assyrian inscriptions give us concerning the Hittites, to which we can attach a date, is met with in the annals of Tiglath-pileser I.

Tiglath-pileser I was the most famous monarch of the first Assyrian empire, and he reigned about 1110 B.C. He carried his arms northward and

westward, penetrating into the bleak and trackless
mountains of Armenia, and forcing his way as far
as Malatiyeh in Kappadokia. His annals present
us with a very full and interesting picture of the
geography of these regions at the time of his reign.
Kummukh or Komagênê, which at that epoch
extended southward from Malatiyeh in the direction of Carchemish, was one of the first objects of
his attack. "At the beginning of my reign," he
says, " 20,000 Moschians (or men of Meshech) and
their five kings, who for fifty years had taken
possession of the countries of Alzi and Purukuzzi,
which had formerly paid tribute and taxes to Assur
my lord—no king (before me) had opposed them
in battle—trusted to their strength, and came
down and seized the land of Kummukh." The
Assyrian king, however, marched against them,
and defeated them in a pitched battle with great
slaughter, and then proceeded to carry fire and
sword through the cities of Kummukh. Its ruler
Kili-Tesup, the son of Kali-Tesup, was captured
along with his wives and family ; and Tiglath-
pileser next proceeded to besiege the stronghold
of Urrakhinas. Its prince Sadi-Tesup, the son
of Khattukhi, the Hittite, threw himself at the
conqueror's feet ; his life was spared, and " the

wide-spreading land of Kummukh " became tributary to Assyria, objects of bronze being the chief articles it had to offer. About the same time, 4,000 troops belonging to the Kaskâ and the people of Uruma, both of whom are described as " soldiers of the Hittites " and as having occupied the northern cities of Mesopotamia, submitted voluntarily to the Assyrian monarch, and were transported to Assyria along with their chariots and their property. Uruma was the Urima of classical geography, which lay on the Euphrates a little to the north of Birejik, so that we know the exact locality to which these " Hittite soldiers " belonged. In fact, " Hittite " must have been a general name given to the inhabitants of all this district, and is extended by the Vannic inscriptions as far north as Malatiyeh.

Tiglath-pileser attacked Kummukh a second time, and on this occasion penetrated still further into the mountain fastnesses of the Hittite country. In a third campaign his armies came in sight of Malatiyeh itself, but the king contented himself with exacting a small yearly tribute from the city, " having had pity upon it," as he tells us, though more probably the truth was that he found himself unable to take it by storm. But he never suc-

ceeded in forcing his way across the fords of the
Euphrates, which were commanded by the great
fortress of Carchemish. Once he harried the
land of Mitanni or Mesopotamia, slaying and
spoiling " in one day " from Carchemish southwards to a point that faced the deserts of the nomad
Sukhi, the Shuhites of the Book of Job. It was
on this occasion that he killed ten elephants in the
neighbourhood of Harran and on the banks of
the Khabour, besides four wild bulls which he
hunted with arrows and spears " in the land of
Mitanni and in the city of Araziqi,[1] which lies
opposite to the land of the Hittites."

Towards the end of the twelfth century before
our era, therefore, the Hittites were still strong
enough to keep one of the mightiest of the Assyrian
kings in check. It is true that they no longer
obeyed a single head ; it is also true that that
portion of them which was settled in the land of
Kummukh was overrun by the Assyrian armies,
and forced to pay tribute to the Assyrian invader.
But Carchemish compelled the respect of Tiglath-
pileser ; he never ventured to approach its walls
or to cross the river which it was intended to
defend. His way was barred to the west, and

---

[1] Called Eragiza in classical geography and in the Talmud.

he never succeeded in traversing the high road which led to Phœnicia and Palestine.

After the death of Tiglath-pileser I the Assyrian inscriptions fail us. His successors allowed the empire to fall into decay, and more than two hundred years elapsed before the curtain is lifted again. These two hundred years had witnessed the rise and fall of the kingdom of David and Solomon as well as the growth of a new power, that of the Syrians of Damascus.

Damascus rose on the ruins of the empire of Solomon. But its rise also shows plainly that the power of the Hittites in Syria was beginning to wane. Hadad-ezer, king of Zobah, the antagonist of David, had been able to send for aid to the Aramæans of Naharina, on the eastern side of the Euphrates (2 Sam. x. 16), and with them he had marched to Helam, in which it is possible to see the name of Aleppo.[1] It is clear that the Hittites were no longer able to keep the Aramæan population in subjection, or to prevent an Aramæan prince of Zobah from expelling them from the territory they had once made their own. Indeed, it may be that in one passage of the Old Testament

---

[1] Called Khalman in the Assyrian texts. Josephus changes Helam into the proper name Khalaman.

allusion is made to an attack which Hadad-ezer
was preparing against them. When it is stated
that he was overthrown by David, " as he was
going to turn his hand against the river Euphrates "
(2 Sam. viii. 3), it may be that it was against the
Hittites of Carchemish that his armies were about
to be directed. At any rate, support for this view
is found in a further statement of the sacred historian. " When Toi king of Hamath," we learn,
" heard that David had smitten all the host of
Hadad-ezer, then Toi sent Joram his son unto
king David, to salute him, and to bless him,
because he had fought against Hadad-ezer and
smitten him : for Hadad-ezer had wars with Toi "
(2 Sam. viii. 9, 10). Now we know from the
monuments that have been discovered on the spot
that Hamath was once a Hittite city, and there is
no reason for not believing that it was still in the
possession of the Hittites in the age of David. Its
Syrian enemies would in that case have been the
same as the enemies of David, and a common
danger would thus have united it with Israel in an
alliance which ended only in its overthrow by the
Assyrians.

As late as the time of Uzziah, we are told by the
Assyrian inscriptions, the Jewish king was in

league with Hamath, and the last independent
ruler of Hamath was Yahu-bihdi, a name in which
we recognise that of the God of Israel. Indeed,
the very fact that the Syrians imagined that " the
kings of the Hittites " were coming to the rescue
of Samaria, when besieged by the forces of Damascus, goes to show that Israel and the Hittites were
regarded as natural friends, whose natural adversaries were the Aramæans of Syria. As the power
and growth of Israel had been built up on the conquest and subjugation of the Semitic populations
of Palestine, so too the power of the Hittites had
been gained at the expense of their Semitic neighbours. The triumph of Syria was a blow alike to
the Hittites of Carchemish and to the Hebrews of
Samaria and Jerusalem.

With Assur-natsir-pal, whose reign extended
from B.C. 885 to 860, contemporaneous Assyrian
history begins afresh. His campaigns and conquests rivalled those of Tiglath-pileser I, and
indeed exceeded them both in extent and in bru-
tality. Like his predecessor, he exacted tribute
from Kummukh as well as from the kings of the
country in which Malatiyeh was situated ; but
with better fortune than Tiglath-pileser he succeeded in passing the Euphrates, and obliging

Sangara of Carchemish to pay him homage. It is
clear that Carchemish was no longer as strong as it
had been two centuries before, and that the power
of its defenders was gradually vanishing away.
There was still, however, a small Hittite population on the eastern bank of the Euphrates ; at
all events, Assur-natsir-pal describes the tribe of
Bakhian on that side of the river as Hittite, and it
was only after receiving tribute from them that
he crossed the stream in boats and approached
the land of Gargamis or Carchemish. But his
threatened assault upon the Hittite stronghold
was bought off with rich and numerous presents.
Twenty talents of silver—the favourite metal of
the Hittite princes—" cups of gold, chains of gold,
blades of gold, 100 talents of copper, 250 talents
of iron, images of copper in the form of wild bulls,
bowls of copper, libation cups of copper, a ring of
copper, the multitudinous furniture of the royal
palace, of which the like was never received,
couches, thrones and plates of rare woods and
ivory, 200 slave-girls, garments of variegated
cloth and purple linen, precious stones, the tusks
of elephants, a white chariot, small images of
gold," as well as ordinary chariots and war-horses,
—such were the treasures poured into the lap of

the Assyrian monarch by the wealthy but unwar-like king of Carchemish. They give us an idea of the wealth to which the city had attained through its favourable position on the high-road of commerce that ran from the east to the west. The uninterrupted prosperity of several centuries had filled it with merchants and riches ; in later days we find the Assyrian inscriptions speaking of " the maneh of Carchemish " as one of the recognized standards of value. Carchemish had become a city of merchants, and no longer felt itself able to oppose by arms the trained warriors of the Assyrian king.

Quitting Carchemish, Assur-natsir-pal pursued his march westwards, and after passing the land of Akhanu on his left, fell upon the town of Azaz near Aleppo, which belonged to the king of the Khat-inians. The latter people were of Hittite descent, and occupied the country between the river Afrin and the shores of the Gulf of Antioch. The Assyrian armies crossed the Afrin and appeared before the walls of the Khattinian capital. Large bribes, however, induced them to turn away southward, and to advance along the Orontes in the direction of the Lebanon. Here Assur-natsir-pal received the tribute of the Phœnician cities.

Shalmaneser III, the son and successor of Assur-natsir-pal, continued the warlike policy of his father (B.C. 860–825). The Hittite princes were again a special object of attack. Year after year Shalmaneser led his armies against them, and year after year did he return home laden with spoil. The aim of his policy is not difficult to discover. He sought to break the power of the Hittite race in Syria, to possess himself of the fords across the Euphrates and the high-road which brought the merchandise of Phœnicia to the traders of Nineveh, and eventually to divert the commerce of the Mediterranean to his own country. By the overthrow of the Khattinians he made himself master of the cedar forests of Amanus, and his palaces were erected with the help of their wood. Sangara of Carchemish, it is true, perceived his danger, and a league of the Hittite princes was formed to resist the common foe. Contingents came not only from Kummukh and from the Khattinians, but from Cilicia and the mountain ranges of Asia Minor. It was, however, of no avail. The Hittite forces were driven from the field, and their leaders were compelled to purchase peace by the payment of tribute. Once more Carchemish gave up its gold and silver, its bronze and copper, its purple vestures and curiously-adorned thrones, and the daughter of Sangara himself was carried away to the harem of the Assyrian king. Pethor, the city of Balaam, was turned into an Assyrian colony, its very name being changed to an Assyrian one. The way into Hamath and Phœnicia at last lay open to the Assyrian host. At Aleppo Shalmaneser offered sacrifices to the native god Hadad, and then descended upon the cities of Hamath. At Karkar he was met by a great confederacy formed by the kings of Hamath and Damascus, to which Ahab of Israel had contributed 2,000 chariots and 10,000 men. But nothing could withstand the onslaught of the Assyrian veterans. The enemy were scattered like chaff, and the river Orontes was reddened with their blood. The battle of Karkar (in B.C. 854) brought the Assyrians into contact with Damascus, and caused Jehu on a later occasion to send tribute to the Assyrian king.

The subsequent history of Shalmaneser concerns us but little. The power of the Hittites south of the Taurus had been broken for ever. The Semite had avenged himself for the conquest of his country by the northern mountaineers centuries before. They no longer formed a barrier which cut off the east from the west, and prevented the Semites of

Assyria and Babylon from meeting the Semites of Phœnicia and Palestine. The intercourse which had been interrupted in the age of the nineteenth dynasty of Egypt could now be again resumed. Carchemish ceased to command the fords of the Euphrates, and was forced to acknowledge the supremacy of the Assyrian invader. In fact, the Hittites of Syria had become little more than tributaries of the Assyrian monarch. When an insurrection broke out among the Khattinians, in consequence of which the rightful king was killed and his throne seized by an usurper, Shalmaneser claimed and exercised the right to interfere. A new sovereign was appointed by him, and he set up an image of himself in the capital city of the Khattinian people.

The change that had come over the relations between the Assyrians and the Hittite population is marked by a curious fact. From the time of Shalmaneser onwards the name of Hittite is no longer used by the Assyrian writers in a correct sense. It is extended so as to embrace all the inhabitants of Northern Syria on the western side of the Euphrates, and subsequently came to include the inhabitants of Palestine as well. Khatta or " Hittite " became synonymous with Syrian. How this happened is not difficult to explain. The first populations of Syria with whom the Assyrian armies come into contact were of Hittite origin. When their power was broken, and the Assyrian armies had forced their way past the barrier they had so long presented to the invader, it was natural that the states next traversed by the Assyrian generals should be supposed also to belong to them. Moreover, many of these states were actually dependent on the Hittite princes, though inhabited by an Aramæan people. The Hittites had imposed their yoke upon an alien race of Aramæan descent, and accordingly in Northern Syria Hittite and Aramæan cities and tribes were intermingled together. " I took," says Shalmaneser, " what the men of the land of the Hittites had called the city of Pethor (*Pitru*), which is upon the river Sajur (*Sagura*), on the further side of the Euphrates, and the city of Mudkinu, on the eastern side of the Euphrates, which Tiglath-pileser (I), the royal forefather who went before me, had united to my country, and Assur-irba king of Assyria and the king of the Aramæans had taken (from it) by a treaty." At a later date Shalmaneser marched from Pethor to Aleppo, and there offered sacrifices to " the god of the city," Hadad-Rimmon, whose name betrays the Semitic character of its population. The Hittites, in short, had never been more than a conquering upper class in Syria, like the Normans in Sicily ; and as time went on the subject population gained more and more upon them. Like all similar aristocracies, they tended to die out or to be absorbed into the native population of the country.

They still held possession of Carchemish, however, and the decadence of the first Assyrian empire gave them an unexpected respite. But the revolution which placed Tiglath-pileser III on the throne of Assyria, in B.C. 725, brought with it the final doom of Hittite supremacy. Assyria entered upon a new career of conquest, and under its new rulers established an empire which extended over the whole of Western Asia. In B.C. 717 Carchemish finally fell before the armies of Sargon, and its last king Pisiris became the captive of the Assyrian king. Its trade and wealth passed into Assyrian hands, it was colonized by Assyrians and placed under an Assyrian satrap. The great Hittite stronghold on the Euphrates. which had been for so many centuries the visible sign of their power and southern conquests, became once more the possession of a Semitic people. The long struggle that had been carried on between the Hittites and the Semites was at an end ; the Semite had triumphed, and the Hittite was driven back into the mountains from whence he had come.

But he did not yield without a struggle. The year following the capture of Carchemish saw Sargon confronted by a great league of the northern peoples, Meshech, Tubal, Melitene and others, under the leadership of the king of Ararat. The league, however, was shattered in a decisive battle, the king of Ararat committed suicide, and in less than three years Komagênê was annexed to the Assyrian empire. The Semite of Nineveh was supreme in the Eastern world.

Ararat was the name given by the Assyrians to the district in the immediate neighbourhood of Lake Van, as well as to the country to the south of it. It was not until post-Biblical days that the name was extended to the north, so that the modern Mount Ararat obtained a title which originally belonged to the Kurdish range in the south. But Ararat was not the native name of the country. This was Biainas or Bianas, a name which still survives in that of Lake Van. Numerous inscriptions are scattered over the country, written in cuneiform characters borrowed from Nineveh in the time of Assur-natsir-pal or his son Shalmaneser, but in a language which bears no resemblance to that of Assyria. They record the building of temples and palaces, the offerings made to the gods, and the campaigns of the Vannic kings. Among the latter mention is made of campaigns against the Khâte or Hittites.

The first of these campaigns was conducted by a king called Menuas, who reigned in the ninth century before our era. He overran the land of Alzi, and then found himself in the land of the Hittites. Here he plundered the cities of Surisilis and Tarkhi-gamas, belonging to the Hittite prince Sada-halis, and captured a number of soldiers, whom he dedicated to the service of his god Khaldis. On another occasion he marched as far as the city of Malatiyeh, and after passing through the country of the Hittites, caused an inscription commemorating his conquests to be engraved on the cliffs of Palu. Palu is situated on the northern bank of the Euphrates, about midway between Malatiyeh and Van, and as it lies to the east of the ancient district of Alzi, we can form some idea of the exact geographical position to which the Hittites of Menuas must be assigned. His son

A SLAB FOUND AT MERASH (*see page* 75).

AN INSCRIPTION FOUND AT CARCHEMISH (*see page* 166).
(*Now destroyed.*)

and successor, Argistis I, again made war upon them, and we gather from one of his inscriptions that the city of Malatiyeh was itself included among their fortresses. The "land of the Hittites," according to the statements of the Vannic kings, stretched along the banks of the Euphrates from Palu on the east as far as Malatiyeh on the west.

The Hittites of the Assyrian monuments lived to the south-west of this region, spreading along the banks of the Orontes to Carchemish and Aleppo. The Egyptian records bring them yet further south to Kadesh on the Orontes, while the Old Testament carries the name into the extreme south of Palestine. It is evident, therefore, that we must see in the Hittite tribes fragments of a race whose original seat was in the ranges of the Taurus, but who had pushed their way into the warm plains and valleys of Syria and Palestine. They belonged originally to Asia Minor, not to Syria, and it was conquest only which gave them a right to the name of Syrians. "Hittite" was their true title, and whether the tribes to which it belonged lived in Judah or on the Orontes, at Carchemish or in the neighbourhood of Palu, this was the title under which they

were known. We must regard it as a national
name, which clung to them in all their conquests
and migrations, and marked them out as a peculiar
people, distinct from the other races of the Eastern
world.   It is now time to see what their own
monuments have to tell us regarding them, and
the influence they exercised upon the history of
mankind.

CHAPTER III

THE HITTITE MONUMENTS

IT was a warm and sunny September morning when I left the little town of Nymphi near Smyrna with a strong escort of Turkish soldiers, and made my way to the Pass of Karabel. The Pass of Karabel is a narrow defile, shut in on either side by lofty cliffs, through which ran the ancient road from Ephesos in the south to Sardes and Smyrna in thc north. The Greek historian Herodotos tells us that the Egyptian conqueror Sesostris had left memorials of himself in this place. " Two images cut by him in the rock " were to be seen beside the roads which led " from Ephesos to Phokæa and from Sardes to Smyrna. On either side a man is carved, a little over three feet in height, who holds a spear in the right hand and a bow in the left. The rest of his accoutrement is similar, for it is Egyptian and Ethiopian, and from one shoulder to the other, right across the breast, Egyptian hieroglyphics have been cut which declare : ' I have won this land with my shoulders.' "

These two images were the object of my journey. One of them had been discovered by Renouard in 1839, and shortly afterwards sketched by Texier ; the other had been found by Dr. Beddoe in 1856. But visitors to the Pass in which they were engraved were few and far between ; the cliffs on either side were the favourite haunt of brigands, and thirty soldiers were not deemed too many to ensure my safety. My work of exploration had to be carried on under the shelter of their guns, for more than twenty bandits were lurking under the brushwood above.

The sculpture sketched by Texier had subsequently been photographed by Mr. Svoboda. It represents a warrior whose height is rather more than life-size, and who stands in profile with the right foot planted in front of him, in the attitude of one who is marching. In his right hand he holds a spear, behind his left shoulder is slung a bow, and the head is crowned with a high peaked cap. He is clad in a tunic which reaches to the knees, and his feet are shod with boots with turned-up ends. The whole figure is cut in deep relief in an artificial niche, and between the spear and the face are three lines of hieroglyphic characters. The figure faces south, and is carved on the face of the eastern cliff of Karabel.

It had long been recognized that the hieroglyphics were not those of Egypt, and Professor Perrot had also drawn attention to the striking resemblance between the style of art represented by this sculpture and that represented by certain rock-sculptures in Kappadokia, as well as by the sculptured image of a warrior discovered by himself at a place called Ghiaur-kalessi, " the castle of the infidel," in Phrygia, which is practically identical in form and character with the sculptured warrior of Karabel.

What was the origin of this art, or who were the people it commemorated, was a matter of uncertainty. A few weeks, however, before my visit to the Pass of Karabel, I announced [1] that I had come to the conclusion that the art was Hittite, and that the hieroglyphics accompanying the figure at Karabel would turn out, when carefully examined, to be Hittite also. The primary purpose of my visit to the pass was to verify this conclusion.

Let us now see how I had arrived at it. The story is a long one, and in order to understand it,

[1] In the *Academy* of August 16, 1879.

it is necessary to transport ourselves from the Pass of Karabel in Western Asia Minor to Hamah, the site of the ancient Hamath, in the far east. It was here that the first discovery was made which has led by slow degrees to the reconstruction of the Hittite empire, and a recognition of the important part once played by the Hittites in the history of the civilized world.

As far back as the beginning of the present century (in 1812) the great Oriental traveller Burckhardt had noticed a block of black basalt covered with strange-looking hieroglyphics built into the corner of a house in one of the bazaars of Hamah.[1] But the discovery was forgotten, and the European residents in Hamah, like the travellers who visited the city, were convinced that " no antiquities " were to be found there. Nearly sixty years later, however, when the American Palestine Exploration Society was first beginning its work, the American consul, Mr. Johnson, and an American missionary, Dr. Jessup, accidentally lighted again upon this stone, and further learned that three other stones of similar character, and inscribed with similar hieroglyphics, existed elsewhere in Hamah. One of them, of

[1] *Travels in Syria*, p. 146.

very great length, was believed to be endowed with healing properties. Rheumatic patients, Mohammedans and Christians alike, were in the habit of stretching themselves upon it, in the firm belief that their pains would be absorbed into the stone. The other inscribed stones were also regarded with veneration, which naturally increased when it was known that they were being sought after by the Franks ; and the two Americans found it impossible to see them all, much less to take copies of the inscriptions they bore. They had to be content with the miserable attempts at reproducing them made by a native painter, one of which was afterwards published in America. The publication served to awaken the interest of scholars in the newly discovered inscriptions, and efforts were made by Sir Richard Burton and others to obtain correct impressions of them. All was in vain, however, and it is probable that the fanaticism or greed of the people of Hamah would have successfully resisted all attempts to procure trustworthy copies of the texts, had not a lucky accident brought Dr. William Wright to the spot. It is to his energy and devotion that the preservation of these precious relics of Hittite literature may be said to be due. " On the 10th of November, 1872," he tells us, he " set out from Damascus, intent on securing the Hamah inscriptions. The Sublime Porte, seized by a periodic fit of reforming zeal, had appointed an honest man, Subhi Pasha, to be governor of Syria. Subhi Pasha brought a conscience to his work, and, not content with redressing wrongs that succeeded in forcing their way into his presence, resolved to visit every district of his province, in order that he might check the spoiler and discover the wants of the people. He invited me to accompany him on a tour to Hamah, and I gladly accepted the invitation." Along with Mr. Green, the English Consul, accordingly, Dr. Wright joined the party of the Pasha ; and, fearing that the same fate might befall the Hamath stones as had befallen the Moabite Stone, which had been broken into pieces to save it from the Europeans, persuaded him to buy them, and send them as a present to the Museum at Constantinople. When the news became known in Hamah, there were murmurings long and deep against the Pasha, and it became necessary, not only to appeal to the cupidity and fear of the owners of the stones, but also to place them under the protection of a guard of soldiers the night before the work of removing them was to commence.

The night was an anxious one to Dr. Wright ; but when day dawned the stones were still safe, and the labour of their removal was at once begun. It " was effected by an army of shouting men, who kept the city in an uproar during the whole day. Two of them had to be taken out of the walls of inhabited houses, and one of them was so large that it took fifty men and four oxen a whole day to drag it a mile. The other stones were split in two, and the inscribed parts were carried on the backs of camels to the " court of the governor's palace. Here they could be cleaned and copied at leisure and in safety.

But the work of cleaning them from the accumulated dirt of ages occupied the greater part of two days. Then came the task of making casts of the inscriptions, with the help of gypsum which some natives had been bribed to bring from the neighbourhood. At length, however, the work was completed, and Dr. Wright had the satisfaction of sending home to England two sets of casts of these ancient and mysterious texts, one for the British Museum, the other for the Palestine Exploration Fund, while the originals themselves were safely deposited in the Museum of Constantinople. It was now time to inquire what the inscriptions meant, and who could have been the authors of them.

Dr. Wright at once suggested that they were the work of the Hittites, and that they were memorials of Hittite writing. But his suggestion was buried in the pages of a periodical better known to theologians than to Orientalists, and the world agreed to call the writing by the name of Hamathite. It specially attracted the notice of Dr. Hayes Ward of New York, who discovered that the inscriptions were written in *boustrophedon* fashion, that is to say, that the lines turned alternately from right to left and from left to right, like oxen when plowing a field, the first line beginning on the right and the line following on the left. The lines read, in fact, from the direction towards which the characters look.

Dr. Hayes Ward also made another discovery. In the ruins of the great palace of Nineveh Sir A. H. Layard had discovered numerous clay impressions of seals once attached to documents of papyrus or parchment. The papyrus and parchment have long since perished, but the seals remain, with the holes through which the strings passed that attached them to the original deeds. Some of the seals are Assyrian, some Phœnician, others again are Egyptian, but there are a few which have upon them strange characters such as had never been met with before. It was these characters which Dr. Hayes Ward perceived to be the same as those found upon the stones of Hamah, and it was accordingly supposed that the seals were of Hamathite origin.

In 1876, two years after the publication of Dr. Wright's article, of which I had never heard at the time, I read a Paper on the Hamathite inscriptions before the Society of Biblical Archæology. In this I put forward a number of conjectures, one of them being that the Hamathite hieroglyphs were the source of the curious syllabary used for several centuries in the island of Cyprus, and another that the hieroglyphs were not an invention of the early inhabitants of Hamath, but represented the system of writing employed by the Hittites. We know from the Egyptian records that the Hittites could write, and that a class of scribes existed among them, and, since Hamath lay close to the borders of the Hittite kingdoms, it seemed reasonable to suppose that the unknown form of script discovered on its site was Hittite rather than Hamathite. The conjecture was confirmed almost immediately afterwards by the discovery of the site of Carchemish, the great Hittite capital, and of inscriptions there in the same system of writing as that found on the stones of Hamah.

It was not long, therefore before the learned world began to recognize that the newly discovered script was the peculiar possession of the Hittite race. Dr. Hayes Ward was one of the first to do so, and the Trustees of the British Museum determined to institute excavations among the ruins of Carchemish. Meanwhile notice was drawn to a fact which showed that the Hittite characters, as we shall now call them, were employed, not only at Hamath and Carchemish, but in Asia Minor as well.

More than a century ago a German traveller had observed two figures carved on a wall of rock near Ibreez, or Ivris, in the territory of the ancient Lykaonia. One of them was a god, who carried in his hand a stalk of corn and a bunch of grapes, the other was a man, who stood before the god in an attitude of adoration. Both figures were shod with boots with upturned ends, and the deity wore a tunic that reached to his knees, while on his head was a peaked cap ornamented with hornlike ribbons. A century elapsed before the sculpture was again visited by a European traveller, and it was again

SLABS WITH HITTITE SCULPTURES.

(Photographed in situ at Keller, near Aintab.)

a German who found his way to the spot. On this occasion a drawing was made of the figures, which was published by Ritter in his great work on the geography of the world. But the drawing was poor and imperfect, and the first attempt to do adequate justice to the original was made by the Rev. E. J. Davis in 1875. He published his copy, and an account of the monument, in the *Transactions of the Society of Biblical Archæology* the following year. He had noticed that the figures were accompanied by what were known at the time as Hamathite characters. Three lines of these were inserted between the face of the god and his uplifted left arm, four lines more were engraved behind his worshipper, while below, on a level with an aqueduct which fed a mill, were yet other lines of half-obliterated hieroglyphs. It was plain that in Lykaonia also, where the old language of the country still lingered in the days of St. Paul, the Hittite system of writing had once been used.

Another stone inscribed with Hittite characters had come to light at Aleppo. Like those of Hamath, it was of black basalt, and had been built into a modern wall. The characters upon it were worn by frequent attrition, the people of Aleppo believing that whoever rubbed his eyes upon it would be immediately cured of ophthalmia. More than one copy of the inscription was taken, but the difficulty of distinguishing the half-obliterated characters rendered the copies of little service, and a cast of the stone was about to be made when news arrived that the fanatics of Aleppo had destroyed it. Rather than allow its virtue to go out of it—to be stolen, as they fancied, by the Europeans—they preferred to break it in pieces. It is one of the many monuments that have perished at the very moment when their importance first became known.

This, then, was the state of our knowledge in the summer of 1879. We knew that the Hittites, with whom Hebrews and Egyptians and Assyrians had once been in contact, possessed a hieroglyphic system of writing, and that this system of writing was found on monuments in Hamath, Aleppo, Carchemish, and Lykaonia. We knew, too, that in Lykaonia it accompanied figures carved out of the rock in a peculiar style of art, and represented as wearing a pecular kind of dress.

Suddenly the truth flashed upon me. This peculiar style of art, this peculair kind of dress, was the same as that which distinguished the sculptures of Karabel, of Ghiaur-kalessi, and of Kappadokia. In all alike we had the same characteristic features, the same head-dresses and shoes, the same tunics, the same clumsy massiveness of design and characteristic attitude. The figures carved upon the rocks of Karabel and Kappadokia must be memorials of Hittite art. The clue to their origin and history was at last discovered; the birthplace of the strange art which had produced them was made manifest. A little further research made the fact doubly sure. The photographs Professor Perrot had taken of the monuments of Boghaz Keui in Kappadokia included one of an inscription in ten or eleven lines. The characters of this inscription were worn and almost illegible, but not only were they in relief, like the characters of all other Hittite inscriptions known at the time, among them two or three hieroglyphs stood out clearly, which were identical with those on the stones of Hamath and Carchemish. All that was needed to complete the verification of my discovery was to visit the Pass of Karabel, and see whether the hieroglyphs Texier and others had found there likewise belonged to the Hittite script.

More than three hours did I spend in the niche wherein the figure is carved which Herodotos believed was a likeness of the Egyptian Sesostris.

It was necessary to take " squeezes " as well as copies, if I would recover the characters of the inscription and ascertain their exact forms. My joy was great at finding that they were Hittite, and that the conclusion I had arrived at in my study at home was confirmed by the monument itself. The Sesostris of Herodotos turned out to be, not the great Pharaoh who contended with the Hittites of Kadesh, but a symbol of the far-reaching power and influence of his mighty opponents. Hittite art and Hittite writing, if not the Hittite name, were proved to have been known from the banks of the Euphrates to the shores of the Ægean Sea.

The stone warrior of Karabel stands in his niche in the cliff at a considerable height above the path, and the direction in which he is marching is that which would have led him to Ephesos and the Mæander. His companion lies below, the block of stone out of which the second figure has been carved having been apparently shaken by an earthquake from the rocks above. This second figure is a duplicate of the first. Both stand in the same position, both are shod with the same snow-shoes, and both are armed with spear and bow. But the second figure has suffered much from the

THE PSEUDO-SESOSTRIS, CARVED ON THE ROCK IN THE PASS OF KARABEL.

ill-usage of man. The upper part has been pur-
posely chipped away, and it is not many years ago
since a Yuruk's tent was pitched against the block
of stone out of which it is carved, the niche in
which the old warrior stands conveniently serving
as the fire-place of the family. No trace of inscription remains, if indeed it ever existed. At
any rate, it could not have run across the breast,
as Herodotos asserts.

The account, indeed, given by Herodotos of
these two figures can hardly have been that of an
eye-witness. Instead of being little over three
feet in height, they are more than life-size, and they
hold their spears not in the right but in the left
hand. Their accoutrement, moreover, is as unlike
that of an " Egyptian and Ethiopian " as it well
could be, while the inscription is not traced
across the breast, but between the face and the arm.
Nor was the Greek historian correct in saying
that the pass which the two warriors seem to guard
leads not only from Ephesos to Phokæa, but also
from Sardes to Smyrna. It is not until the pass is
cleared at its northern end that the road which
runs through it—the *Karabeldéré*, as the Turks
now call it—joins the *Belkaive*, or road from Sardes
to Smyrna. It is evident that Herodotos must

have received his account of the figures from another authority, though his identification of them with the Egyptian Sesostris is his own.

Not far from Karabel another monument of Hittite art has been discovered. Hard by the town of Magnesia, on the lofty cliffs of Sipylos, a strange figure has been carved out of the rock. It represents a woman with long locks of hair streaming down her shoulders, and a jewel like a lotus-flower upon the head, who sits on a throne in a deep artificial niche. Lydian historians narrate that it was the image of the daughter of Assaon, who had sought death by casting herself down from a precipice ; but Greek legend preferred to see in it the figure of " weeping Niobê " turned to stone. Already Homer told how Niobê, when her twelve children had been slain by the gods, " now changed to stone, broods over the woes the gods had brought, there among the rocks, in lonely mountains, even in Sipylos, where they say are the couches of the nymphs who dance on the banks of the Akheloios." But it was only after the settlement of the Greeks in Lydia that the old monument on Mount Sipylos was held to be the image of Niobê. The limestone rock out of which it was carved dripped with moisture after rain, and as the water flowed over the face of the figure, disintegrating and disfiguring the stone as it ran, the pious Greek beheld in it the Niobê of his own mythology. The figure was originally that of the great goddess of Asia Minor, known sometimes as Atergatis or Derketo, sometimes as Kybelê, sometimes by other names. It is difficult for one who has seen the image of Nofert-ari, the favourite wife of Ramses II, seated in the niche of rock on the cliffs of Abusimbel, not to believe that the artist who carved the image on Mount Sipylos had visited the Nile. At a little distance both have the same appearance, and a nearer examination shows that, although the Egyptian work is finer than the Lydian, it resembles it in a striking manner. We now know, however, that the " Niobê " of Sipylos owes its origin to Hittite art. On the wall of rock out of which the niche is cut wherein the goddess sits Dr. Dennis discovered a cartouche containing Hittite characters. By tying some ladders together he and I succeeded in ascending to it, and taking paper impressions of the hieroglyphs. Among them is a character which has the meaning of " king." [1]

[1] A copy of the inscription made from the squeeze is given in the *Transactions of the Society of Biblical Archæology*, VII, Pt. 3,

How came these characters and these creations of Hittite art in a region so remote from that in which the Hittite kingdoms rose and flourished ? How comes it that we find figures of Hittite warriors in the Pass of Karabel and on the rocks of Ghiaur-kalessi, and the image of a Hittite goddess on the cliffs of Sipylos ? Whose was the hand that en-graved the characters that accompany them—characters which are the same as those which meet us on the stones of Hamath and Carchemish ? We have now to learn what answers can be given to these questions.

Pl. v.   An eye-copy, made from the ground by Dr. Dennis, on the occasion of his discovery of the cartouche, was published in the *Proceedings* of the same Society for January, 1881, and is necessarily imperfect.

CHAPTER IV

THE HITTITE EMPIRE

WE have seen that the Egyptian monuments bear witness to an extension of Hittite power into the distant regions of Asia Minor. When the kings of Kadesh contended with the great Pharaoh of the Oppression they were able to summon to their aid allies from the Troad, as well as from Lydia and the shores of the Cilician sea. A century later Egypt was again invaded by a confederacy, consisting partly of the Hittite rulers of Carchemish and Aleppo, partly of Libyans and Teukrians, and other populations of Asia Minor. If any trust can be placed in the identifications proposed by Egyptian scholars for the countries from whence the vassals and allies of the Hittites came it is clear that memorials of Hittite power and conquest ought to be found in Asia Minor.

And they were found as soon as it was recognized that the curious monuments of Asia Minor, of which the warriors of Karabel and the sculptures of Ibreez are examples, were actually inspired by

Hittite art. As soon as it was known that the art these monuments represented, and the peculiar form of writing which accompanied them, had their earliest home in the Syrian cities of the Hittite tribes, a new light broke over the pre-historic past of Asia Minor. These Hittite monuments can be traced in two continuous lines from Northern Syria and Kappadokia to the western extremity of the peninsula. They follow the two highways which once led out of Asia to Sardes and the shores of the Ægean. In the south they form as it were a series of stations at Ibreez and Bulgar Maden in Lykaonia, at Fassiler and Tyriaion between Ikonion and the Lake of Beyshehr, and finally in the Pass of Karabel. Northwards the line runs through the Taurus by Merash, and carries us first to the defile of Ghurun, and then to the great Kappadokian ruins of Boghaz Keui and Eyuk, from whence we pass by Ghiaur-kalessi and the burial-place of the old Phrygian kings, until we again reach the Lydian capital and the Pass of Karabel.

Westward of the Halys and Kappadokia they are marked by certain peculiarities. They are found either in the vicinity of silver mines, like those of Lykaonia, or else on the line of the ancient roads, which finally converged in Lydia. None have been discovered in the central plateau of Asia Minor, in the mountains of Lykia in the south, or the wide-reaching coast-lands of the north. They mark the sites of small colonies, or else the lines of road that connected them. Moreover, with the exception of the image of the goddess who sits on her throne in Mount Sipylos, the western monuments represent the figures of warriors who are in the act of marching forward. This is the case at Karabel; it is also the case at Ghiaur-kalessi, where the rock on which the two Hittite warriors are carved lies close below the remains of a prehistoric fortress.

Such facts admit of only one explanation. The Hittite monuments of Western Asia Minor must be memorials of military conquest and supremacy. In the warriors whose figures stood on either side of the Pass of Karabel, the sculptor must have seen the visible symbols of Hittite power. They showed that the Hittite had won and kept the pass by force of arms. They are emblems of conquest, not creations of native art.

But it was inevitable that conquest should bring with it a civilizing influence. The Hittites could not carry with them the art and culture they had

acquired in the East without influencing the barbarous populations over whom they claimed to
rule. The vassal chieftains of Lydia and the
Troad could not lead their forces unto Syria, or
assist in the invasion of Egypt, without learning
something of that ancient civilization with which
they had come in contact. The Hittites, in fact,
must be regarded as the first teachers of the rude
populations of the West. They brought to them
a culture the first elements of which had been
inspired by Babylonia ; they brought also a system
of writing out of which, in all probability, the
natives of Asia Minor afterwards developed a
writing of their own.

It is possible, therefore, that some of the Hittite
monuments of Asia Minor are the work, not of the
Hittites themselves, but of the native populations
whom they have civilized and instructed. It may
be that this is the case at Ibreez, where the faces
of the god and his worshipper have Jewish features
very unlike those found on monuments of purely
Hittite origin. But apart from such instances,
where the monument is due to Hittite influence
rather than to Hittite artists, it is certain that most
of the Hittite memorials of Asia Minor are the
productions of the Hittites themselves. This is

MONUMENT OF A HITTITE KING FOUND AT CARCHEMISH.

proved by the hieroglyphs which are attached to them, as well as by the uniform type of feature and dress which prevails from Carchemish to the Ægean. It is impossible to explain such a uniformity, and still more the extraordinary resemblance between the characters engraved at Karabel, or on Mount Sipylos, and those which meet us in the inscriptions of Hamath and Carchemish, except on the supposition that the monuments were executed by men who belonged to the same race and spoke the same language. Wherever Hittite inscriptions occur, we find in them the same combinations of hieroglyphs as well as the use of the same characters to denote grammatical suffixes.

We may, then, rest satisfied with the conclusion that the existence of a Hittite empire extending into Asia Minor is certified, not only by the records of ancient Egypt, but also by Hittite monuments which still exist. In the days of Ramses II, when the children of Israel were groaning under the tasks allotted to them, the enemies of their oppressors were already exercising a power and a domination which rivalled that of Egypt. The Egyptian monarch soon learned to his cost that the Hittite prince was as " great " a king as himself, and could summon to his aid the inhabitants of the unknown north. Pharaoh's claim to sovereignty was disputed by adversaries as powerful as the ruler of Egypt, if indeed not more powerful, and there was always a refuge among them for those who were oppressed by the Egyptian king.

When, however, we speak of a Hittite empire we must understand clearly what that means. It was not an empire like that of Rome, where the subject provinces were consolidated together under a central authority, obeying the same laws and the same supreme head. It was not an empire like that of the Persians, or of the Assyrian successors of Tiglath-pileser III, which represented the organized union of numerous states and nations under a single ruler. Such a conception of empire was due to Tiglath-pileser III, and his successor Sargon ; it was a new idea in the world, and had never been realized before. The first Assyrian empire, like the foreign empire of Egypt, was of an altogether different character. It depended on the military enterprise and strength of individual monarchs. As long as the Assyrian or Egyptian king could lead his armies into distant territories, and compel their inhabitants to pay him tribute and homage, his empire extended over them. But hardly had he returned home laden with spoil than we find the subject populations throwing off their allegiance and asserting their independence, while the death of the conqueror brought with it almost invariably the general uprising of the tribes and cities his arms had subdued. Before the days of Tiglath-pileser, in fact, empire in Western Asia meant the power of a prince to force a foreign people to submit to his rule. The conquered provinces had to be subdued again and again ; but as long as this could be done, as long as the native struggles for freedom could be crushed by a campaign, so long did the empire exist.

It was an empire of this sort that the Hittites established in Asia Minor. How long it lasted we cannot say. But so long as the distant races of the West answered the summons to war of the Hittite princes, it remained a reality. The fact that the tribes of the Troad and Lykia are found fighting under the command of the Hittite kings of Kadesh, proves that they acknowledged the supremacy of their Hittite lords, and followed them to battle like the vassals of some feudal chief. If Hittite armies had not marched to the shores of the Ægean, and Hittite princes been able from time to time to exact homage from the nations of the far west, Egypt would not have had to contend against the

populations of Asia Minor in its wars with the
Hittites, and the figures of Hittite warriors would
not have been sculptured on the rocks of Karabel.
There was a time when the Hittite name was
feared as far as the western extremity of Asia
Minor, and when Hittite satraps had their seat in
the future capital of Lydia.

Traditions of this period lingered on into
classical days. The older dynasty of Lydian kings
traced its descent from Bel and Ninos, the Babylonian or Assyrian gods, whose names had been
carried by the Hittites into the remote west. The
Lydian hero Kayster, who gave his name to the
Kaystrian plain, was fabled to have wandered into
Syria, and there, after wooing Semiramis, to have
been the father of Derketo, the goddess of Carchemish. A Lydian was even said to have drowned
Derketo in the sacred lake of Ashkelon ; and
Eusebius declares that Sardes, the Lydian capital,
was captured for the first time in B.C. 1078, by a
horde of invaders from the north-western regions
of Asia.

But it is in the famous legend of the Amazons
that we must look for the chief evidence preserved
to us by classical antiquity of the influence once
exercised by the Hittites in Asia Minor. The

Amazons were imagined to be a nation of female warriors, whose primitive home lay in Kappadokia, on the banks of the Thermodon, not far from the ruins of Boghaz Keui. From hence they had issued forth to conquer the people of Asia Minor and to found an empire which reached to the Ægean Sea. The building of many of the most famous cities on the Ægean coast was ascribed to them,—Myrina and Kyme, Smyrna and Ephesos, where the worship of the great Asiatic goddess was carried on with barbaric ceremonies into the later age of civilized Greece.

Now these Amazons are nothing more than the priestesses of the Asiatic goddess, whose cult spread from Carchemish along with the advance of the Hittite armies. She was served by a multitude of armed priestesses and eunuch priests ; under her name of Ma, for instance, no less than six thousand of them waited on her at Komana in Kappadokia. Certain cities, in fact, like Komana and Ephesos, were dedicated to her service, and a large part of the population accordingly became the armed ministers of the mighty goddess. Generally these were women, as at Ephesos in early days, where they obeyed a high-priestess, who called herself " the queen-bee." When Ephesos passed into Greek hands, the goddess worshipped there was identified with the Greek Artemis, and a high-priest took the place of the high-priestess. But the priestess of Artemis still continued to be called " a bee," reminding us that Deborah or " Bee " was the name of one of the greatest of the prophetesses of ancient Israel ; and the goddess herself continued to be depicted under the same form as that which had belonged to her in Hittite days. On her head was the so-called mural crown, the Hittite origin of which has now been placed beyond doubt by the sculptures of Boghaz Keui, while her chariot was drawn by lions. It was from the Hittites, too, that Artemis received her sacred animal, the goat.

The " spear-armed host " of the Amazons, which came from Kappadokia, which conquered Asia Minor, and was so closely connected with the worship of the Ephesian Artemis, can be no other than the priestesses of the Hittite goddess, who danced in her honour armed with the shield and bow. In ancient art the Amazons are represented as clad in the Hittite tunic and brandishing the same double-headed axe that is held in the hands of some of the Hittite deities on the rocks of Boghaz Keui, while the " spear " lent to them by the Greek poet brings to our recollection the spear held by the warriors of Karabel. We cannot explain the myth of the Amazons except on the supposition that they represented the armed priestesses of the Hittite goddess, and that a tradition of the Hittite empire in Asia Minor has entwined itself around the story of their arrival in the West. The cities they are said to have founded must have been the seats of Hittite rule.

The Hittites were intruders in Syria as well as in Western Asia Minor. Everything points to the conclusion that they had descended from the ranges of the Taurus. Their costume was that of the inhabitants of a cold and mountainous region, not of the warm valleys of the south. In place of the trailing robes of the Syrians, the national costume was a tunic which did not quite reach to the knees. It was only after their settlement in the Syrian cities that they adopted the dress of the country; the sculptured rocks of Asia Minor represent them with the same short tunic as that which distinguished the Dorians of Greece or the ancient inhabitants of Ararat. But the most characteristic portion of the Hittite garb was the shoes with upturned ends. Wherever the figure of a Hittite is portrayed, there we find this peculiar form of boot. It reappears among the hieroglyphs of the inscriptions, and the Egyptian artists who adorned the walls of the Ramesseum at Thebes have placed it on the feet of the Hittite defenders of Kadesh. The boot is really a snow-shoe, admirably adapted for walking over snow, but ill-suited for the inhabitants of a level or cultivated country. The fact that it was still used by the Hittites of Kadesh in the warm fertile valley of the Orontes proves better than any other argument that they must have come from the snow-clad mountains of the north. It is like the shoe of similar shape which the Turks have carried with them in their migrations from the north and introduced amongst the natives of Syria and Egypt. It indicates with unerring certainty the northern origin of the Turkish conqueror. He stands in the same relation to the modern population of Syria that the Hittites stood to the Aramæans of Kadesh three thousand years ago.

Equally significant is the long fingerless glove which is one of the most frequent of Hittite hieroglyphs. The thumb alone is detached from the rest of the bag in which the fingers were enclosed. Such a glove is an eloquent witness to the wintry cold of the regions from which its wearers came, and a similar glove is still used during the winter months by the peasants of modern Kappadokia.

We may find another evidence of the northern descent of the Hittite tribes in the hieroglyph which is used in the sense of " country." It represents two, or sometimes three, pointed mountains, whose forms, as was remarked some years ago, resemble those of the mountains about Kaisariyeh, the Kappadokian capital.

If we leave Kadesh and proceed northwards, the local names bear more and more the peculiar stamp of a Hittite origin. We leave Semitic names like Kadesh, " the sanctuary," behind us, and at length find ourselves in a district where the geographical names no longer admit of a Semitic etymology. It is just this district, moreover, in which Hittite inscriptions first become plentiful. The first met with to the south are the stones of Hamath and the lost inscription of Aleppo ; but from Carchemish northwards we now know that numbers of them still exist. The territory covered by them is a square, the base of which is formed by a line running from Carchemish through Antioch into Lykaonia, while the remains at Boghaz Keui and Eyuk constitute its northern limit. We must regard this region as having been the primæval home and starting-point of the Hittite race. They will have been a population which clustered round the two flanks of the Taurus range, extending far into Kappadokia on the north, and towards Armenia on the east.

They preserved their independence on the banks of the Halys in Kappadokia for nearly two hundred years after the fall of Carchemish. It was not long before the overthrow of Lydia by Cyrus that Krœsos, the Lydian king, destroyed the cities of Pteria, where the ruins of Boghaz Keui and Eyuk now stand, and enslaved their inhabitants, thus avenging upon them the conquest of his own country by their ancestors so many centuries before. Herodotos calls them " Syrians," a name which is qualified as " White Syrians " by the Greek geographer Strabo. It was in this way that the Greek writer wished to distinguish them from the dark-coloured Syrians of Aramæan or Jewish birth, with whom he was otherwise acquainted ; and it reminds us that, whereas the Egyptian artists painted the Hittites with yellow skins, they painted the Syrians with red. It is an interesting fact that the memory of their relationship to the population on the Syrian side of the Taurus should

THE DOUBLE-HEADED EAGLE OF EYUK.

have been preserved so long among these Hittites of Kappadokia.

Boghaz Keui and Eyuk are situated in the district known as Pteria to the Greeks. At Eyuk there are remains of a vast palace, which stood on an artificial platform of earth, like the palaces of Assyria and Babylon. The walls of the palace, formed of huge blocks of cut stone, can still be traced in many places. It was approached by an avenue of sculptured slabs, on which lions were represented, some of them in the act of devouring a ram. The head and attitude of one that is preserved remind us of the avenue of ram-headed sphinxes which led to the temple of Karnak at Thebes. The entrance of the palace was flanked on either side by two enormous monoliths of granite, on the external faces of which were carved in relief the images of a sphinx. But though the artist had clearly gone to Egypt for his model, it is also clear that he had modified the forms he imitated in accordance with national ideas. The head-dress, like the feet, of the sphinxes is non-Egyptian, the necklace passes under the chin instead of falling across the breast, and the sphinx itself is erect, not recumbent, as in Egypt. On the right hand the same block of stone which bears the figure of the sphinx bears also, on the inner side, the figure of a double-headed eagle, with an animal which Professor Perrot believes to be a hare in either talon, and a man standing upon its twofold head. The same double-headed eagle, supporting the figure of a man or a god, is met with at Boghaz Keui, and must be regarded as one of the peculiarities of Hittite symbolism and art. The symbol, whose prototype goes back to primitive Babylonia, was adopted in later days by the Turkoman princes, who had perhaps first seen it on the Hittite monuments of Kappadokia ; and the Crusaders brought it to Europe with them in the fourteenth century. Here it became the emblem of the German emperors, who have passed it on to the modern kingdoms of Russia and Austria. It is not the only heirloom of Hittite art which has descended to us of to-day.

The lintel of the palace gate at Eyuk was of solid stone, and, if Professor Perrot is right, the huge stone lintel, adorned with a lion's head, still lies in fragments on the ground. The entrance was flanked with walls on which bas-reliefs were carved, as in the palaces which were built by the kings of Assyria. They formed, in fact, a dado, the rest of the wall above them being probably of brick covered with stucco and painted with bright colours. Many of the sculptured blocks still lie scattered on the ground. Here we have the picture of a priest before an altar, there of a sacred bull mounted on a pedestal. Hard by is the likeness of two men, one of whom carries a lyre, the other a goat ; while on another stone a man is represented with little regard to perspective in the act of climbing a ladder. Another relief introduces us to three rams and a goat whose horn is grasped by a shepherd ; elsewhere again we see a goddess seated in a chair of peculiar construction, with her feet upon a stool and objects like flowers in her hand. A similar piece of sculpture has been found at Merash, on the southern side of the Taurus, within the limits of the ancient Komagênê, even such details as the form of the chair and stool being alike in the two cases. The two reliefs might have been executed by the same hand.

The sphinxes which guarded the entrance of the palace of Eyuk and the avenue which led up to them bear unmistakable testimony to the influence of Egyptian art upon its builders. They take us back to a period when the Hittites of Kappadokia were in contact with the people of the Nile, and thus confirm the evidence of the Egyptian records. There must have been a time when the population of distant Kappadokia held intercourse with that of Egypt, and this time, as we learn from the Egyptian monuments, was the age of Ramses II. It is perhaps not going too far to assume that the palace of Eyuk was erected in the fourteenth century before our era, and is a relic of the period when the sway of the Hittite princes of Kadesh or Carchemish extended as far north as the neighbourhood of the Halys. It is indeed possible that the palace was originally the summer residence of the kings whose homes were in the south. The plateau on which Eyuk and Boghaz Keui stand is more than 2,000 feet above the level of the sea, and the winters there are intensely cold. From December onwards the ground is piled high with snow. It is well known that the descendants of races which have originally come from a cold climate endure the heats of a southern summer with impatience ; and the same causes which make the English rulers of India to-day retire during the summer to the mountain heights, may have made the Hittite lords of Syria build their summer palace in the Kappadokian highlands.

The sculptures of Boghaz Keui perhaps belong

to a later date than those of Eyuk. Boghaz Keui
is five hours to the south-west of Eyuk, and marks
the site of a once populous town. A stream that
runs past it separates the ruins of the city from a
remarkable series of sculptures carved on the rocks
of the mountains which overlooked the city. The
city was surrounded by a massive wall of masonry,
and within it were two citadels solidly built on the
summits of two shafts of rock. The wall was
without towers, but at its foot ran a moat cut
partly through the rock, partly through the earth,
the earth being coated with a smooth and slippery
covering of masonry. The most important building in the city was the palace, a plan of which has
been made by modern travellers. Like the palace
of Eyuk, it was erected on an artificial mound or
terrace of earth, and its ornamentation seems to
have been similar to that of Eyuk. But little is
left of it save the foundations of the walls and the
overturned throne of stone which once stood in
the central court supported on the bodies of two
lions. Lions' heads were also carved on the
columns which formed the door-posts of the city
gate.

The interest of Boghaz Keui centres in the sculptures which have been carved with so much care on

the rocky walls of the mountains. Here advantage has been taken of two narrow recesses, the sides and floors of which have been artificially shaped and levelled. The first and largest recess may be described as of rectangular shape. Along either side of it, as along the dado of a room, run two long lines of figures in relief, which eventually meet at the end opposite the entrance. On the left-hand side we see a line of men, almost all clad alike in the short tunic, peaked tiara, and boots with upturned ends that characterize Hittite art. At times, however, they are interrupted by other figures in the long Syrian robe, who may perhaps be intended for women. Among them are two dwarf-like creatures upholding the crescent disk of the moon, and after a while the procession becomes that of a number of deities, each with his name written in Hittite hieroglyphs at his side. After turning the corner of the recess, the procession consists of three gods, two of whom stand on mountain-peaks, while the foremost (with a goat beside him) is supported on the heads of two adoring priests. Facing him is the foremost figure of the other procession, which starts from the eastern side of the recess, and finally meets the first on its northern wall. This figure is that of

SCULPTURES AT BOGHAZ KEUI.

the great Asiatic goddess, who wears on her head the mural crown and stands upon a panther, while beside her, as beside the god she is greeting, is the portraiture of a goat. Behind her a youthful god, with the double-headed battle-axe in his hand, stands upon a panther, and behind him again are two goddesses with mural crowns, whose feet rest upon the heads and wings of a double-headed eagle. This eagle, whose form is but a reproduction of that sculptured at Eyuk, closes the series of designs represented on the northern wall. The eastern wall is occupied with a long line, first of goddesses and then of priestesses. Where the line breaks off at last we come upon a solitary piece of sculpture. This is the image of a eunuch-priest, who stands on a mountain and holds in one hand a curved augural wand, in the other a strange symbol representing a priest with embroidered robes, who stands upon a shoe with upturned ends, and supports a winged solar disk, the two extremities of which rest upon baseless columns

The entrance to the second recess is guarded on either side by two winged monsters, with human bodies and the heads of dogs. It leads into an artificially excavated passage of rectangular shape, on the rocky walls of which detached groups of

figures and emblems are engraved. On the western wall is a row of twelve priests or soldiers,
each of whom bears a scythe upon his shoulder ;
facing them on the eastern wall are two reliefs of
strange character. One of them depicts the
youthful god, whose name perhaps was Attys,
embracing with his left arm the enunch-priest,
above whose head is engraved the strange symbol
that has been already described. The other
represents a god's head crowned with the peaked
tiara, and supported on a double-headed lion,
which again stands on the hinder feet of two other
lions, whose heads rest on a column or stem. All
these sculptures were once covered with stucco,
and thus preserved from the action of the weather.

It is evident that in these two mountain recesses
we have a sanctuary, the forms and symbols of
whose deities were sculptured on its walls of living
rock. It was a sanctuary too holy to be confined
within the walls of the city, and the supreme
deities to whom it was dedicated were a god and a
goddess, served by a multitude of male and female
priests. In fact, as Prof. Perrot remarks, Boghaz
Keui must have been a sacred city like Komana,
whose citizens were consecrated to the chief
divinities adored by the Hittites, and were

SCULPTURES AT BOGHAZ KEUI.

governed by a high-priest. It was as much a
" Kadesh " or " Hierapolis," as much a " holy
city," as Carchemish itself.

It is not its sculptures only which prove to us
that it was a city of the Hittites. The figures of
the deities have attached to them, as at Eyuk, the
same hieroglyphs as those which meet us in the
inscriptions of Hamath and Aleppo, of Carchemish and Merash, and within its walls, southward
of the ruins of its palace, Prof. Perrot discovered a
long text of nine or ten lines cut out of the rock,
and though worn and disfigured by time and
weather, still showing the forms of many Hittite
characters. Dr. Belck has succeeded in copying
the first four lines, which contain the same forms
as those which are found on the Hittite monuments
of Syria.

Tedious as all these details may seem to be, it
has been necessary to give them, since they tell us
what was the appearance and construction of a
Hittite city, a Hittite palace, and the interior of a
Hittite temple. The discoveries recently made in
the Hittite districts south of the Taurus show us
that here too the palaces and temples were like
those of Eyuk and Boghaz Keui. Here too we
find the same dados sculptured with the same

figures dressed in the same costume ; here too we meet with the same lions, and the same winged deities standing on the backs of animals. A photograph of a piece of sculpture on a block of basalt at Carchemish, taken by Dr. Gwyther, might have been taken at Boghaz Keui. The art, the forms, and the symbolism are all the same.

At Zinjerli, north of the Gulf of Antioch, a Hittite city and palace have been revealed to us by the excavations of Dr. von Luschan. It is true that the remains belong to an age when the old Hittite town had passed into the hands of Aramæan Semites. But the bulk of the population must still have continued to be Hittite, and the art continued to be so too. Even the inscriptions, though in the letters of the so-called Phœnician alphabet, are carved in relief, like the Hittite texts of an earlier time. The sculptured slabs which lined the walls of the palace can now be studied in the Museum of Berlin ; the figures and costumes, like the mythology they illustrate, are all Hittite, and resemble in both style and subject those of Kappadokia. There are the same composite animals, the same deities, the same mother-goddess seated on her chair and raising the cup to her lips, while the priest sits or stands before the table on which the divine repast is served. The Semitic dynasty which ruled in Samalla or Ya(u)di—for so the land was called of which Zinjerli was the capital—could not long have succeeded one of Hittite descent, and the Hittite names that still lingered in the royal family preserved a memory of the fact.

The high-road from Boghaz Keui to Merash must have passed through the defile of Gurun, where Sir Charles Wilson discovered Hittite inscriptions carved upon the cliff. But there may have been a second road which led through Kaisariyeh, the modern capital of Kappadokia, southward to Bor or Tyana, where Prof. Ramsay found a Hittite text, and from thence to the silver mines of the Bulgar Dagh. The bas-reliefs of Ibreez are not far distant from the famous Cilician gates which led the traveller from the great central plateau of Asia Minor to Tarsus and the sea.

It would seem that the silver mines of the Bulgar Dagh were first worked by Hittite miners. Silver had a special attraction for the Hittite race. The material on which the Hittite version of the treaty between the Hittite king of Kadesh and the Egyptian Pharaoh was written was a tablet of that metal. That such tablets were in frequent use, results from the fact that all the other Hittite inscriptions known to us are not incised, but cut in relief upon the stone. It is therefore obvious that the Hittites must have first inscribed their hieroglyphs upon metal, rather than upon wood or stone or clay ; it is only in the case of metal that it is less laborious to hammer or cast in relief than to cut the metal with a graving tool, and nothing can prove more clearly how long accustomed the Hittite scribes must have been to doing so, than their imitation of this work in relief when they came to write upon stone. It is possible that most of the silver of which they made use came from the Bulgar Dagh. The Hittite inscription found near the old mines of these mountains, proves that they had once occupied the locality. It is even possible that their settlement for a time in Lydia was also connected with their passion for " the bright metal." At all events the Gumush Dagh, or " Silver Mountains," lie to the south of the Pass of Karabel, and traces of old workings can still be detected in them. At how early a date the mines may have been worked can be judged from the fact that Dr. Gladstone's analysis of the gold discovered among the monumental remains of the Sixth Egyptian Dynasty, proved it to have come from Asia Minor. Here only is it mixed with tin in the proportion required by the analysis. More than three thousand years before our era, therefore, there must have been trade between Egypt and Asia Minor, where the mining industry may already have been carried on.

However this may be, the Hittite monuments of Asia Minor confirm in a striking way the evidence of the Egyptian inscriptions. They show us that the Hittites worked for silver in the mountains which looked down upon the Cilician plain, from whence the influence of their art and writing extended into the plain itself. They further show that the central point of Hittite power was a square on either side of the Taurus range, which included Carchemish and Komagênê in the south, the district eastwards of the Halys on the north, and the country of which Malatiyeh was the capital in the east. The Hittite tribes, in fact, were mountaineers from the plateau of Kappadokia who had spread themselves out in all directions. A time came when, under the leadership of powerful princes, they marched along the two high-roads of Asia Minor and established their supremacy over the coast-tribes of the far west. The age to which this military empire belongs is indicated by the Egyptian character of the so-called image of Niobê on the cliff of Sipylos, as well as by the sphinxes which guarded the entrance to the palace of Eyuk. It goes back to the days when the rulers of Kadesh could summon to their aid the vassal-chieftains of the Ægean coast. The monuments the Hittites have left behind them in Asia Minor thus bear the same testimony as the records of Egypt. The people to whom Uriah, and it may be Bathsheba, belonged, not only had contended on equal terms with one of the greatest of Egyptian kings ; they had carried their arms through the whole length of Asia Minor, they had set up satraps in the cities of Lydia, and had brought the civilization of the East to the barbarous tribes of the distant West.

CHAPTER V

THE HITTITE CITIES AND RACE.

OF the history of the "White Syrians" or Hittites who lived in the land of Pteria, near the Halys, we know little at present beyond what we can gather from the excavation of their stronghold at Boghaz Keui and their palace at Eyuk. The same is the case with the Hittite tribes of Malatiyeh and Komagênê. When the inscription which adorns the body of a stone lion found at Merash can be fully deciphered, it will doubtless cast light on the early history of the city ; at present even its ancient name is uncertain. It is not until we leave the mountainous region originally occupied by the Hittite race, and descend into the valleys of Syria, that the annals of their neighbours begin to tell us something about their fortunes and achievements. The history of their two southern capitals, Carchemish and Kadesh, broken and imperfect though it may be, is not an utter blank.

The site of Carchemish had long been looked

for in vain. At one time it was identified with the Kirkesion or Circesium of classical geography, built at the confluence of the Khabour and the Euphrates. But the Assyrian name of Kirkesion was different, and its position did not agree with that assigned to " Gargamis " or Carchemish in the Assyrian texts. Professor Maspero subsequently placed the latter at Membij, the ancient Mabog or Hierapolis, on the strength of the evidence furnished by classical authors and the Egyptian monuments ; but the ruins of Membij contain nothing earlier than the Greek period, and their position on a rocky plateau at a distance from the Euphrates, is inconsistent with the fact known to us from the Assyrian inscriptions, that Carchemish commanded the fords over the Euphrates.

To Mr. Skene, for many years the English consul at Aleppo, is due the credit of first discovering the true site of the old Hittite capital. On the western bank of the Euphrates, midway between Birejik and the mouth of the Sajur, rises an artificial mound of earth, under which ruins and sculptured blocks of stone had been found from time to time. It was known as Jerablûs, or Kalaat Jerablûs, " the fortress of Jerablûs," sometimes wrongly written Jerabîs ; and in the name of

Jerablûs Mr. Skene had no difficulty in recognizing an Arab corruption of Hierapolis. In the Roman age the name of Hierapolis or " Holy City " had been transferred to its neighbour Membij, which inherited the traditions and religious fame of the older Carchemish ; but when the triumph of Christianity in Syria brought with it the fall of the great temple of Membij, the name disappeared from the later city, and was remembered only in connexion with the ruins of the ancient Carchemish.

Two years after Mr. Skene's discovery, Mr. George Smith visited Carchemish on his last ill-fated journey from which he never returned, and recognized at once that Mr. Skene's identification was right. The position of Jerablûs suited the requirements of the Assyrian texts, it lay on the high-road which formerly led from east to west, and among its ruins was an inscription in Hittite characters. Not long afterwards there were brought to the British Museum the bronze bands which once adorned the gates of an Assyrian temple, and on one of these is a picture in relief of Carchemish as it looked in the days of Jehu of Israel. The Euphrates is represented as running past its walls, thus conclusively showing that

Jerablûs, and not Membij, must be the site on which it stood.

The site was bought by Mr. Henderson, Mr. Skene's successor at Aleppo, and the money was invested by the former owner in the purchase of a cow. The mighty were fallen indeed when the Hittite capital which had resisted the armies of Egypt and Assyria was judged to be worth no more than the price of a beast of the field. In 1878 Mr. Henderson was employed by the Trustees of the British Museum in excavating on the spot ; but no sufficient supervision was exercised over the workmen, and though a few remains of Hittite sculpture and writing found their way to London, much was left to be burned into lime by the natives or employed in the construction of a mill.

The ancient city was defended on two sides by the Euphrates, and was exposed only on the north and west. Here, however, an artificial canal had been cut, on either side of which was a fortified wall. The mound which had first attracted Mr. Skene's attention marks the site of the royal palace, where the excavators found the remains of a dado like that of Eyuk, the face of the stones having been sculptured into the likeness of gods and men. The men were shod with boots with upturned ends, that unfailing characteristic of Hittite art.

Carchemish enjoyed a long history. When first we hear of it in the Egyptian records it was already in Hittite hands. Thothmes III fought beneath its walls, and his bravest warriors plunged into the Euphrates in their eagerness to capture the foe. Tiglath-pileser I had seen its walls from the opposite shore of the Euphrates, but had not ventured to approach them. Assur-natsir-pal and his son Shalmaneser had received tribute from its king, and when it finally surrendered to the armies of Sargon it was made the seat of an Assyrian satrap. The trade which had flowed through it continued to pour wealth into the hands of its merchants, and the " maneh of Carchemish " remained a standard of value. When Egypt made her final struggle for supremacy in Asia, it was under the walls of Carchemish that the decisive struggle was fought. The battle of Carchemish in B.C. 604 drove Necho out of Syria and Palestine, and placed the destinies of the chosen people in the hands of the Babylonian king. It is possible that the ruin of Carchemish dates from the battle. However that may be, long before the beginning of the Christian era it had been supplanted by

Mabog or Membij, and the great sanctuary which had made it a " holy city " was transferred to its rival and successor.

Like Carchemish, Kadesh on the Orontes, the most southern capital the Hittites possessed, was also a " holy city." Pictures of it have been preserved on the monuments of Ramses II. We gather from them that it stood on the shore of the Lake of Homs, still called the " Lake of Kadesh," at the point where the Orontes flowed out of the lake. The river was conducted round the city in a double channel, across which a wide bridge was thrown, the space between the two channels being apparently occupied by a wall.

Kadesh must have been one of the last conquests made by the Hittites in Syria, and their retention of it was the visible sign of their supremacy over Western Asia. We do not know when they were forced to yield up its possession to others. As has been pointed out, the correct reading of 2 Sam. xxiv. 6 informs us that the northern limit of the kingdom of David was formed by " the Hittites of Kadesh," " the entering in of Hamath," as it seems to be called elsewhere. In the age of David, accordingly, Kadesh must still have been in their hands, but it had already ceased to be so when the Assyrian king Shalmaneser III led his armies to the west. No allusion to the city and its inhabitants occurs in the Assyrian inscriptions, and we may conjecture that it had been destroyed by the Syrians of Damascus. As Membij took the place of Carchemish, so Emesa or Homs took the place of Kadesh.[1]

Was Hebron also in the south of Palestine a Hittite city ? Already in the days of Abraham we hear of two cities occupying the ground on which the later Hebron stood. One of these is the Amorite Mamre ; the other is Kirjath-Arba, which in the time of the patriarch was inhabited by " the children of Heth." In the children of Heth commentators have agreed to see the Hittites, and their view seems to be supported by the independent testimony of Ezekiel, who makes the Hittites part of the original population of Jerusalem, and whose archæological interests are visible elsewhere in his prophecies. On the other hand, Arba, we are told, the founder of Kirjath-Arba, was " the father of Anak," and the

---

[1] The Kidis or Kadesh mentioned in a Babylonian contract of the fortieth year of Nebuchadrezzar, and published by Dr. Pinches in the *Records of the Past*, new series, iv. pp. 99–101, is not necessarily Kadesh on the Orontes. At any rate the latter had long ceased to be a Hittite town.

references to the Anakim in the Old Testament would lead us to infer that they were either of Amorite descent or survivors of the early neolithic population of Canaan. That they were not Hittites is pretty clear.

Nevertheless we now have documentary evidence that in the Mosaic age, at all events, the Hittites had established themselves in what became later the territory of Judah. We have learned from the Tel el-Amarna tablets that the sons of the Hittite prince Arzawaya had there won land for themselves and seduced the Egyptian governors from their loyalty to the Pharaoh. The letter of Ebed-Khiba, the vassal-king of Jerusalem, in which he recounts the fact, is so important, and has hitherto been so misinterpreted, that I give it here in full :—

" To the king my lords thus [says] Ebed-Khiba thy servant : at the feet of the king my lord seven times seven I [fall]. Behold Melech-el (*Milkilim*) does not separate himself from the sons of Labai (the Bedâwî) and [from] the sons of Arzaya [1] to demand the territory of the king for themselves. As for a governor who has committed such an act, why does not the king call him in question ? Behold Melech-el and Tagi ; the act which they

---

[1] Written Arzawaya and Arzauya elsewhere.

have committed is this : At that time they took it, even the city of Rabbah (*Rubuda*), and now Jerusalem—if this land belongs to the king why (are they trying to seize it) ? When the city of Gaza was appointed for the king,[1] behold the land of the city of Gath-Carmel (*Gimti-kirmil*) was (assigned) to Tagi, and the men of Gath formed a garrison in Beth-Sannah (*Bit-Sâni*, less probably Beth-Shean), and we acted. When they gave Labai and Mount Shechem (*Sakmi*) to the Khabiri (Confederates), Melech-el sent to Tagi, and they took the sons of the house as slaves (?). They granted all their requests to the men of Keilah (*Kelti*). But we will rescue Jerusalem. The garrison which you sent by the hand of Khaya the son of Meri-Ra Hadad-ya has taken. He has put them in his house in Gaza, has sent twenty men to Egypt. There is no garrison of the king with me. May the king live for ever ! If Pa-ur (the royal commissioner) goes down to him [to Egypt, let the king know that] he has separated himself from me (and) is in Gaza, and let the king remember to send him a garrison of fifty men to defend the land. All the king's land is revolting. Send Yekhenkhamu and let

---

[1] By being placed under a special Egyptian Resident.

him look after the king's land.—To the royal
secretary says Ebed-Khiba [thy] servant : [Bring]
the news plainly before the [king]. May it
be abundantly well with you. Thy servant
am I."

We gather from a subsequent part of the correspondence that Jerusalem eventually fell into the
hands of its enemies, among whom the sons of
Arzawaya and their Hittite followers must be
reckoned. We thus have the explanation of
a fact to which I have drawn attention in
The Races of the Old Testament. Among the
ethnological types represented on the Egyptian
monuments, casts of which were made by Prof.
Flinders Petrie for the British Association, are
the heads of the inhabitants of Ashkelon in
the age of the Exodus. These heads present us
with the characteristic features of the Hittite race,
and so bear witness to the existence of a population of the Hittite type in the southern corner of
Palestine.

If Hittite adventurers could find their way to the
south of Canaan at a time when it was still under
the government and protection of Egypt, there is
no reason why they should not have done so centuries before. And the language in which Ezekiel

describes the foundation of Jerusalem implies that such was the case. It was founded as much by Hittites as by Amorites, and since it was already an important city and the capital of a district in the age of the Tel el-Amarna tablets, its Hittite founders must have been in Southern Palestine at an early date. The name of its king Ebed-Khiba, " the servant of the god Khiba," may itself be an evidence of this, if the current reading of the name is right. Khiba was a Mitannian deity, whose name is also found in that of the Hittite queen Putu-Khipa. In Ebed-Khiba, the priest-king of Jerusalem, we may have a descendant of invaders who once poured into the " land of the Amorites " from Mesopotamia and the Hittite lands.

We have seen that the Hittites were originally a northern race. Their primitive home probably lay on the northern side of the Taurus. What they were like we can learn both from their own sculptures and from the Egyptian monuments, which agree most remarkably in the delineation of their features. The extraordianry resemblance between the Hittite faces drawn by the Egyptian artists and those depicted by themselves in their bas-reliefs and their hieroglyphs, is a convincing proof of the faithfulness of the Egyptian representations, as well as of the identity of the Hittites of the Egyptian inscriptions with the Hittites of Carchemish and Kappadokia.

It must be confessed that they were not a handsome people. They were short and thick of limb, and the front part of their faces was pushed forward in a curious and somewhat repulsive way. The forehead retreated, the cheek-bones were high, the nostrils were large, the upper lip protrusive. They had, in fact, according to the craniologists, the characteristics of a Mongoloid race. Like the Mongols, moreover, their skins were yellow and their eyes and hair were black. They arranged the hair in the form of a " pigtail," which characterizes them on their own and the Egyptian monuments quite as much as their snow-shoes with upturned toes.

In Syria they doubtless mixed with the Semitic race, and the further south they advanced the more likely they were to become absorbed into the native population. The Hittites of Southern Judah have Semitic names, and probably spoke a Semitic language. Kadesh continued to bear to the last its Semitic title, and among the Hittite names which occur further north there are several which display a Semitic stamp. In the neighbourhood of Carchemish Hittites and Aramæans were mingled together, and Pethor was at once a Hittite and an Aramæan town. In short, the Hittites in Syria were like a conquering race everywhere; they formed merely the governing and upper class, which became smaller and smaller the further removed they were from their original seats. Like the Normans in Sicily or the Etruscans in ancient Italy, they tended gradually to disappear or else to be absorbed into the subject race. It was only in their primitive homes that they survived in their original strength and purity, and though even in Kappadokia they lost their old languages, adopting in place of them first Aramaic, then Greek, and lastly Turkish, we may still observe their features and characteristics in the modern inhabitants of the Taurus range. Even in certain districts of Kappadokia their descendants may still be met with. " The type," says Sir Charles Wilson, " which is not a beautiful one, is still found in some parts of Kappadokia, especially amongst the people living in the extraordinary subterranean towns which I discovered beneath the great plain north-west of Nigdeh." The characteristics of race, when once acquired, seem almost indelible ; and it is possible that, when careful observations can be made, it will be found that the ancient Hittite race still survives not only in Eastern Asia Minor, but even in the southern regions of Palestine.

CHAPTER VI

HITTITE RELIGION AND ART

LUCIAN, or some other Greek writer who has usurped his name, has left us a minute account of the great temple of Mabog as it existed in the second century of the Christian era. Mabog, as we have seen, was the successor of Carchemish; and there is little reason to doubt that the pagan temple of Mabog, with all the rites and ceremonies that were carried on in it, differed but little from the pagan temple of the older Carchemish.

It stood, we are told, in the very centre of the "Holy City." It consisted of an outer court and an inner sanctuary, which again contained a Holy of Holies, entered only by the high-priest and those of his companions who were "nearest the gods." The temple was erected on an artificial mound or platform, more than twelve feet in height, and its walls and ceiling within were brilliant with gold. Its doors were also gilded, but the Holy of Holies or innermost shrine was not provided with doors, being separated from the rest of the building, it would seem, like the Holy of Holies in the Jewish temple, by a curtain or veil. On either side of the entrance was a cone-like column of great height, a symbol of the goddess of fertility, and in the outer court a large altar of brass. To the left of the latter was an image of " Semiramis," and not far off a great " sea " or " lake," containing sacred fish. Oxen, horses, eagles, bears, and lions were kept in the court, as being sacred to the deities worshipped within.

On entering the temple the visitor saw on his left the throne of the Sun-god, but no image, since the Sun and Moon alone of the gods had no images dedicated to them. Beyond, however, were the statues of various divinities, among others the wonder-working image of a god who was believed to deliver oracles and prophecies. At times, it was said, the image moved of its own accord, and if not lifted up at once by the priests, began to perspire. When the priests took it in their hands, it led them from one part of the temple to the other, until the high-priest, standing before it, asked it questions, which it answered by driving its bearers forward. The central objects of worship, however, were the golden images of two deities, whom Lucian identifies with the Greek Hera and Zeus, another figure standing between them, on the head of which rested a golden dove. The goddess, who blazed with precious stones, bore in her hand a sceptre and on her head that turreted or mural crown which distinguishes the goddesses of Boghaz Keui. Like them, moreover, she was supported on lions, while her consort was carried by bulls. In him we may recognize the god who at Boghaz Keui is advancing to meet the supreme Hittite goddess.

In the Egyptian text of the treaty between Ramses and the king of Kadesh, the supreme Hittite god is called Sutekh, the goddess being Antarata, the Semitic Ashtoreth. In later days, however, the goddess of Carchemish was known as Athar-'Ati, which the Greeks transformed into Atargatis and Derketo. Derketo was fabled to be the mother of Semiramis, in whom Greek legend saw an Assyrian queen ; but Semiramis was really the goddess Istar, called Ashtoreth in Canaan, and Atthar or Athar by the Aramæans, among whom Carchemish was built. Derketo was, therefore, but another form of Semiramis, or rather but another name under which the great Asiatic goddess was known. The dove was sacred to her, and this explains why an image of the dove was placed above the head of the third image in the divine triad of Mabog.

The temple was served by a multitude of priests. More than 300 took part in the sacrifices on the day when Lucian saw it. The priests were dressed in white, and wore the skull-cap which we find depicted on the Hittite monuments. The high-priest alone carried on his head the lofty tiara, which the sculptures indicate was a prerogative of gods and kings. Prominent among the priests were the Galli or eunuchs, who on the days of festival cut their arms and scourged themselves in honour of their deities. Such actions remind us of those priests of Baal who "cut themselves after their manner with knives and lancets, till the blood gushed out upon them."

Twice a year a solemn procession took place to a small chasm in the rock under the temple, where, it was alleged, the waters of the deluge had been swallowed up, and water from the sea was poured into it. It is to this pit that Melito, a Christian writer of Syria, alludes when he says that the goddess Simi, the daughter of the supreme god Hadad, put an end to the attacks of a demon by filling with sea water the pit in which he lived. But in Lucian's time the demon was regarded as the deluge, and the account of the deluge given to the Greek writer agrees so closely with that which we read in Genesis as to make it clear that it had been borrowed by the priests of Hierapolis from the Hebrew Scriptures. It is probable, however, that the tradition itself was of much older standing, and had originally been imported from Babylonia. At all events the hero of the deluge was called Sisythes, a modification of the name of the Chaldæan Noah, while Major Conder found a place in the close neighbourhood of Kadesh which is known as " the Ark of the Prophet Noah," and close at hand a spring termed the Tannur or " Oven," out of which, according to Mohammedan belief, the waters of the flood gushed forth.

But there were many other festivals at Mabog besides that which commemorated the subsidence of the deluge. Pilgrims flocked to it from all parts —Arabia, Palestine, Kappadokia, Babylonia, even India. They were required to drink water only, and to sleep on the ground. Numerous and rich were the offerings which they brought to the shrine, and once arrived there were called upon to offer sacrifices. Goats and sheep were the most common victims, though oxen were also offered. The only animal whose flesh was forbidden to be either sacrificed or eaten was the swine ; as among the Jews, it was regarded as unclean. After being dedicated in the court of the temple the animal was usually led to the house of the offerer, and there put to death ; sometimes, however, it was killed by being thrown from the entrance to the temple. Even children were sacrificed by their parents in this way, after first being tied up in skins and told that they were " not children but oxen."

Different stories were current as to the foundation of the temple. There were some who affirmed that Sisythes had built it after the deluge over the spot where the waters of the flood had been swallowed up by the earth. It is possible that this was the legend originally believed in Mabog before the traditions of Carchemish had been transferred to it. It seems to be closely connected with the local peculiarities of the site. The other legends had doubtless had their origin in the older Hierapolis. According to one of them, the temple had been founded by Semiramis in honour of her mother Derketo, half woman and half fish, to whom the fish in the neighbouring lake were sacred. Another account made Attys its founder, and the goddess to whom it was dedicated the divinity called Rhea by the Greeks.

Derketo and Rhea, however, are but different names of the same deity, who was known as Kybelê or Kybêbê in Phrygia, and honoured with the title of " the Great Mother." Her images were covered with breasts, to symbolize that she was but mother-earth, from whom mankind derived their means of life. Her attributes were borrowed from those of the Babylonian Istar, the Ashtoreth of Canaan; even the form assigned to her was that of the Babylonian Istar, as we learn from a bas-relief discovered at Carchemish, where she is represented as naked, a lofty tiara alone excepted, with the hands upon the breasts and a wing rising behind each shoulder. She was, in fact, a striking illustration of the influence exerted upon the Hittites, and through them upon the people of Asia Minor, by Babylonian religion and worship. Even in Lydia a stone has been found on which her image is carved in a rude style of art, but similar in form to the representations of her in the bas-relief of Carchemish and the cylinders of ancient Chaldæa.

This stone, like the seated figure on Mount Sipylos, is a witness that her cult was carried westward by the Hittite armies. Later tradition preserved a reminiscence of the fact. The Lydian hero Kayster was said to have gone to Syria, and there had Derketo for his bride, while on the other hand it was a Lydian, Mopsos, who was believed to have drowned the goddess Derketo in the sacred lake of Ashkelon. We have here, it may be, recollections of the days when Lydian soldiers marched against Egypt under the leadership of Hittite princes, and learnt to know the name and the character of Athar-'Ati, the goddess of Carchemish.

The Babylonian Istar was accompanied by her son and bridegroom Tammuz, the youthful Sun-god, the story of whose untimely death made a deep impression on the popular mind. Even in Jerusalem Ezekiel saw the women weeping for the death of Tammuz within the precincts of the temple itself ; and for days together each year in the Phœnician cities the festival of his death and resurrection were observed with fanatic zeal. In Syria he was called Hadad, and identified with the god Rimmon, so that Zechariah (xii. 11) speaks of the mourning for Hadad-Rimmon in the valley of Megiddo. At Hierapolis and Aleppo also he was known as Hadad or Dadi, while throughout Asia Minor he was adored under the name of Attys, " the shepherd of the bright stars." The myth which told of his death underwent a slight change of form among the Hittites, and through them among the tribes of Asia Minor. He is doubtless the young god who on the rocks of Boghaz Keui appears behind the mother-goddess, riding like her on the back of a panther or lion.

The people of Mabog did not forget that their temple was but the successor of an older one, and that Carchemish had once been the " Holy City " of Northern Syria. The legends, therefore, which referred to the foundation of the sanctuary were said to relate to one which had formerly existed, but had long since fallen into decay. The origin of the temple visited by Lucian was ascribed to a certain " Stratonikê, the wife of the Assyrian king." But Stratonikê is merely a Greek trans-formation of some Semitic epithet of "Ashtoreth," and marks the time when the Phœnician Ashtoreth took the place of the earlier Athar-'Ati. A strange legend was told of the youthful Kombabos, who was sent from Babylon to take part in the building of the shrine. Kombabos was but Tammuz under another name, just as Stratonikê was Istar, and the legend is chiefly interesting as testifying to the religious influence once exercised by the Baby-lonians upon the Hittite people.

Semiramis may turn out to have been the Hittite name of the goddess called Athar-'Ati by the Aramæan inhabitants of Hierapolis. In this case the difficulty of accounting for the existence of the two names would have been solved in the old myths by making her the daughter of Derketo. But while Derketo was a fish-goddess, Semiramis was associated with the dove, like the Ashtoreth or Aphrodite who was worshipped in Cyprus. The symbol of the dove had been carried to the distant West at an early period. Among the objects found by Dr. Schliemann in the prehistoric tombs of Mykenæ were figures in gold-leaf, two of which represented a naked goddess with the hands upon the breasts and doves above her, while the third has the form of a temple, on the two pinnacles of which are seated two doves. Considering how intimately the prehistoric art of Mykenæ seems to have been connected with that of Asia Minor, it is hardly too much to suppose that the symbol of the dove had made its way across the Ægean through the help of the Hittites, and that in the pinnacled temple of Mykenæ, with its two doves, we may see a picture of a Hittite temple in Lydia or Kappadokia.

The legends reported by Lucian about the

foundation of the temple of Mabog all agreed that it was dedicated to a goddess. The " Holy City " was under the protection, not of a male but of a female divinity, which explains why it was that it was served by eunuch priests. If Attys or Hadad was worshipped there, it was in right of his mother ; the images of the other gods stood in the temple on sufferance only. The male deity whom the Greek author identified with Zeus must have been regarded as admitted by treaty or marriage to share in the honours paid to her. It must have been the same also at Boghaz Keui. Here, too, the most prominent figure in the divine procession is that of the Mother-goddess, who is followed by her son Attys, while the god who is the Zeus of Lucian advances to meet her.

In Cilicia and Lydia this latter god seems to have been known as Sandan. He is called on coins the " Baal of Tarsos," and he carries in his hand a bunch of grapes and a stalk of corn. We may see his figure engraved on the rock of Ibreez. Here he wears on his head the pointed Hittite cap, ornamented with horn-like ribbons, besides the short tunic and boots with upturned ends. On his wrists are bracelets, and earrings hang from his ears.

Sandan was identified with the Sun, and hence it happened that when a Semitic language came to prevail in Cilicia he was transformed into a supreme Baal. The same transformation had taken place centuries before in the Hittite cities of Syria. Beside the Syrian goddess Kadesh, who is represented as standing upon a lion, like the great goddess of Carchemish, the Egyptian monuments tell us of Sutekh, who stands in the same relation to his Hittite worshippers as the Semitic Baal stood to the populations of Canaan. Sutekh was the supreme Hittite god, but at the same time he was localized in every city or state in which the Hittites lived. Thus there was a Sutekh of Carchemish and a Sutekh of Kadesh, just as there was a Baal of Tyre and a Baal of Tarsos. The forms under which he was worshipped were manifold, but everywhere it was the same Sutekh, the same national god.

It would seem that the power of Sutekh began to wane after the age of Ramses, and that the goddess began to usurp the place once held by the god. It is possible that this was due to Babylonian and Assyrian influence. At any rate, whereas it is Sutekh who appears at the head of the Hittite states in the treaty with Ramses, in later days the

chief cult of the " Holy Cities " was paid to the
Mother-goddess. His place was taken by the
goddess at Carchemish as well as at Mabog, at
Boghaz Keui as well as at Komana.

In the Kappadokian Komana the goddess went
under the name of Ma. She was served by 6,000
priests and priestesses, the whole city being dedicated to her service. The place of the king was
occupied by the Abakles or high-priest. We have
seen that the sculptures of Boghaz Keui give us
reason to believe that the same was also the case
in Pteria ; we know that it was so in other " Holy
cities " of Asia Minor. At Pessinus in Phrygia,
where lions and panthers stood beside the goddess,
the whole city was given up to her worship under
the command of the chief Gallos or priest ; and
on the shores of the Black Sea the Amazonian
priestesses of Kybelê, who danced in armour in
her honour, were imagined by the Greeks to
constitute the sole population of an entire country.
At Ephesos, in spite of the Greek colony which
had found its way there, the worship of the Mother-
goddess continued to absorb the life of the inhabitants, so that it still could be described in the time
of St. Paul as a city which was " a worshipper of
the great goddess." Here, as at Pessinus, she was

worshipped under the form of a meteoric stone " which had fallen from heaven."

We may regard these " Holy Cities," placed under the protection of a goddess and wholly devoted to her worship, as peculiarly characteristic of the Hittite race. Their two southern capitals, Kadesh and Carchemish, were cities of this kind, and their stronghold at Boghaz Keui was presumably also a consecrated place. Their progress through Asia Minor was characterized by the rise of priestly cities and the growth of a class of armed priestesses. Komana in Kappadokia, and Ephesos on the shores of the Ægean, are typical examples of such holy towns. The entire population ministered to the divinity to whom the city was dedicated, the sanctuary of the deity stood in its centre, and the chief authority was wielded by a high-priest. If a king existed by the side of the priest, he came in course of time to fill a merely subordinate position.

These " Holy Cities " were also " Asyla " or Cities of Refuge. The homicide could escape to them, and be safe from his pursuers. Once within the precincts of the city and the protection of its deity, he could not be injured or slain. But it was not only the man who had slain another by accident who could thus claim an " asylum " from his enemies. The debtor and the political refugee were equally safe. Doubtless the right of asylum was frequently abused, and real criminals took advantage of regulations which were intended to protect the unfortunate in an age of lawlessness and revenge. But the institution on the whole worked well, and, while it strengthened the power of the priesthood, it curbed injustice and restrained violence.

Now the institution of Cities of Refuge did not exist only in Asia Minor and in the region occupied by the Hittites. It existed also in Palestine, and it seems not unlikely that it was adopted by the great Hebrew lawgiver, acting under divine guidance, from the older population of the country. The Hebrew cities of refuge were six in number. One of them was " Kedesh in Galilee," whose very name declares it to have been a " Holy City," like Kadesh on the Orontes, while another was the ancient sanctuary of Hebron, once occupied by Hittites and Amorites. Shechem, the third city of refuge on the western side of the Jordan, had been taken by Jacob " out of the hand of the Amorite " (Gen. xlviii. 22) ; and the other three cities were all on the eastern side of the Jordan, in the region so long held by Amorite tribes. We are therefore tempted to ask whether these cities had not already been " asyla " or cities of refuge long before Moses was enjoined by God to make them such for the Israelitish conquerors of Palestine.

The names of several of the Hittite deities may be recovered from the names of individuals into whose composition they enter. Sandes or Sandan, Tarqu or Tarkhu, Saba and Rhô are thus known to us, as well as others which it is not needful to specify. The cuneiform tablets discovered by the Germans at Boghaz Keui have revealed a multitude of gods and goddesses, as well as subordinate spirits embodied in the sacred bulls, at the head of whom stood the god Tessub. Saba, under the adjectival form of Sabazios, has been made familiar to us by Greek writers. Sabazios was identified sometimes with Zeus, sometimes with Dionysos, and his priests, who adopted the dress and name of the god, were called the Sabi. The serpent, we are told, was sacred to him, perhaps the stag as well.

Now a Hittite seal in the possession of Dr. Hayes Ward has upon it the names of Sandan and the goddess of Carchemish, with the figure of a priest standing in front of the symbol of the divine pair. The symbol is a curious one, for it represents a coiled snake whose head is that of a stag. It must, therefore, have been under this compound emblem that the divinities who watched over the destinies of the Hittite capital were imaged.

It would seem indeed that there was a time when the Hittite gods were not as yet portrayed in human form. It was in Babylonia that the gods were first represented as men, and this conception of the divinity doubtless first made its way to Asia Minor along with the other elements of Babylonian culture and art. But the older conception was never altogether forgotten. Even at Boghaz Keui, along with the deities who are sculptured in the likeness of man, we find the sacred dirk with its hilt formed of four heraldic lions surmounted by a high-priest's head. The deities themselves are made to stand upon the animals sacred to them, which were once the gods whose symbols they became. The goat of Tarku, the lion of Kybelê, were once Tarku and Kybelê themselves. It is probable that the determinative of " deity " in the Hittite hieroglyphs is the picture of a sacred stone wrapped in cloths. Such sacred stones continued to be revered down to the latest days of Asianic heathenism; the

" great goddess " of Ephesos was a meteorite that had " fallen from heaven."

With the introduction of Babylonian art, however, came a new conception of the divine. The deities of Hittite and Asianic faith put on human shape, and it is in this shape that we usually see them depicted on the monuments of Hittite art. Perhaps the way was prepared by the adoption of Babylonian deities under Babylonian names. An Assyro-Babylonian colony was settled but a little eastward of Kaisariyeh, in the very heart of the Hittite region, at an early period, and local names like that of the river Saros, or words like that by which the high-priest of Komana was known, show how thoroughly Babylonian civilization must have permeated the Hittite tribes. Already in the treaty between Ramses II and his Hittite rivals mention is made of Askhir, " the mistress of the mountains," and Askhir is the Babylonian Iskhara, whose name appears on a bilingual Hittite and cuneiform seal now in the Ashmolean Museum. What she was like is shown us on another seal on which her Hittite name alone is written. Here she sits in woman's dress and with a horned cap on her head, holding in her hand at one time a goat, at another time a dove and a trident, while the winged solar

disk is engraved above her. At Fraktin in Kappadokia we again find the seated goddess with the
dove before her ; but here it is " the goddess of
heaven " that is represented with the high-priest
standing in front dressed like the goddess herself.

At times the goddesses wear the mural crowns
which denoted the walls of a city. The Hittite city
or tribe was deified, and the city and its guardian
goddess accordingly bore the same name. Hence
it is that Hittite princes had names like Khattusil
and Khalipasil, where the city name, Khattu-sas,
means " belonging to Khattu." It is a repetition
of what meets us in Assyria, where Assur was the
god of the state as well as the state itself.

That the mural crown should have been given to
the goddess rather than to the god is explained by
the prominent position assigned to her in Hittite
religion. The primary object of worship was the
mother-goddess. Along with the god, her husband,
and her son, she formed a triad found throughout
Asia Minor, however various the names under
which the several members of it were known. At
Boghaz Keui, as we have seen, the god stands on
the bowed heads of two priests, with a crowned
goat at his side, while the goddess faces him, also
with a goat at the side and standing on a panther's

back. Behind her is her son, the Attys of the classical writers, carrying in his hand the double-headed battle-axe and standing like his mother on a panther's back. Two goddesses, supported on the wings of a double-headed eagle, constitute his rear-guard.

The inscriptions at Gurun on the Tokhma-Su are dedicated by the king of Carchemish to the divine triad. The name of the god comes first, and is represented by the same hieroglyph as that which is used to express it at Boghaz Keui. The goddess, however, is not designated by the name she bears at Boghaz Keui, but by the symbol which her image, brought from Carchemish to the British Museum, carries in her left hand. Here, too, in her right hand is the battle-axe, the emblem of conquest and power. Both at Gurun and at Boghaz Keui Attys is denoted by the picture of the lower limbs of a man.

A fragment of Cilician mythology has been preserved to us in the geographical dictionary of Stephanus of Byzantium. We gather from it that the Hittite deities were believed to have been the children of the Earth and Sky, a natural conclusion indeed, when we remember that so many of them were deified towns or countries, and that according

to the treaty between Ramses and the Hittites the
Hittite rivers were also divine. In fact, Stephanus
tells us that both the city of Adana and the river
Saros were gods. The mother-goddess represented
the Earth, while the god was the Sky, though there
was also a " queen of heaven " who presided over
" all the gods."

By the side of the primitive triad the Sun-god
too was adored. He was, it is true, often identified
with the supreme god or his son, but this was in
the later days of religious philosophizing. Thus
Sandan, or Sandes, the divine husbandman of
Cilicia whom the Greeks transformed into their
Heraklês, was at times confounded with the Sun-
god, and in Syria we even find him replaced by
the Semitic Hadad. But the Hadad worshipped
at Aleppo was rather that youthful Sun-god whose
death was mourned by weeping women, than the
Sun-god who wielded the thunder-bolt, causing
the corn to ripen and the grape to mature.

Closely connected with Hittite religion was
Hittite art. Religion and art have been often inter-
twined together in the history of the world, and
we can often infer the religion of a people from its
art, as in the case of the sculptures of Boghaz Keui.
Hittite art was a modification of that of Babylonia,

and bears testimony to the same Babylonian influence as the worship of the " Mother-goddess."
The same Chaldæan culture is presupposed by
both.

But while the art of the Hittites was essentially
Babylonian in origin, it was profoundly modified
in the hands of the Hittite artists. The deities,
indeed, were made to ride on the backs of animals,
as upon Babylonian cylinders, the walls of the
palaces were adorned with long rows of bas-reliefs,
as in Chaldæa and Assyria, and there was the same
tendency to arrange animals face to face in heraldic
style ; but nevertheless the workmanship and the
details introduced into it were purely native. Even
a symbol like the winged solar disk assumes in
Hittite sculpture a special character which can
never be mistaken. The Hittite artist excelled in
the representation of animal forms, but the lion,
which he seems to have never wearied of designing,
is treated in a peculiar way which marks it sharply
off from the sculptured lions either of Babylonia
or of any other country. So, too, in the case of
the human figure, though the general conception
has been derived from Babylonian art, the conception is worked out in a new and original manner.
Those who have once seen the sculptured image

of a Hittite warrior or a Hittite god, can never confuse it with the artistic productions of another race. The figure is clearly drawn from the daily experience of the sculptor's own life. The dress with its peaked shoes, the thick rounded form, the strange protrusive profile, were copied from the costume and appearance of his fellow countrymen, and the striking agreement that exists between his representation of them and that which we find on the Egyptian monuments proves how faithfully he must have worked. The elements, in short, of Babylonian art are present in the art of the Hittite, but the treatment and selection are his own.

It is in his selection and combination of these elements that he exhibits most clearly his originality. Monsters, half human, half bestial, were known to the Babylonians, but it was left to the Hittites to invent a double-headed eagle, or to plant a human head on a column of lions. The winged horse, again, the Pegasus of Greek mythology, was a Hittite invention, and we find it engraved on Hittite seals, while the Chimæra seems equally to go back to a Hittite prototype. The so-called rope-pattern occurs once or twice on Babylonian gems, but it became a distinguishing characteristic of Hittite art, like the employment of the heads only of animals instead of their entire forms.

So, again, the heraldic arrangement of animals face to face, or more rarely back to back, had its first home in Chaldæa, but it was the Hittites who raised it into a principle of art. We may perhaps trace their doing so to their love of animal forms.

The influence of Babylonian culture may have made itself first felt in the age of the eighteenth Egyptian dynasty, when the cuneiform tablets of Tel el-Amarna represent the Hittite tribes as descending southward into the Syrian plains. It may on the other hand go back to a much earlier epoch. We have no materials at present for deciding the question. One fact, however, is clear ; there was a time when the Hittites were profoundly affected by Babylonian civilization, religion, and art. Before this could have been the case they must have been already in contact with Syria.

It is more easy to fix the period when the Hittite sculptor received that inspiration from Egyptian art which produced the sphinxes of Eyuk and the seated image on Mount Sipylos. It can only have been the age of Ramses II, and of the great wars between Egypt and the Hittite princes in the four-

teenth century before our era. The influence of
Egypt was but transitory, but it was to it, in all
probability, that the Hittites owed the idea of
hieroglyphic writing.

At a far later date Babylonian influence was
superseded by that of Assyria. The later sculptures of Carchemish betray the existence of Assyrian rather than of Babylonian models. The
winged figure of the goddess of Carchemish now
in the British Museum is Assyrian in style and
character, and it is possible that other draped
images of the goddess may be derived from the
same source. In Babylonian art Istar was represented nude.

Among the ruins of the palace of Milid, the
capital of the ancient Melitene, bas-reliefs have
been found which reflect the Assyrian art of the
age of Assurnatsir-pal. The king is represented
in his chariot, hunting in one case a lion, which
turns back to roar at him, in another case a stag.
By the side of the king stands the driver, while
underneath the horse runs a dog. The chariot,
with its six-spoked wheel, is drawn by one horse
only, and the weapons used by the king are a bow
and arrows. But the whole design is Assyrian
in character: it is only its clumsiness of execu-

tion that declares it to be the work of a foreign sculptor.

To Professor Perrot we owe the discovery of bronze figures of Hittite manufacture. The execution of them is at once conventional and barbarous. Nothing can exceed the rudeness of a figure now in the Louvre, which represents a god with a pointed tiara, standing on the back of an animal. Though the face of the god has evidently been modelled with care, it is impossible to tell to what zoological species the animal which supports him is intended to belong. Almost equally far removed from nature is the bronze image of a bull which is also in the Louvre.

If these bronzes are to be regarded as the highest efforts of Hittite metallurgic work, it is not to be regretted that they are few in number. But it is quite different with the engraved gems which we now know to have been of Hittite workmanship. Many of them are exceedingly fine ; a hæmatite cylinder, for instance, which was discovered at Kappadokia, is equal to the best products of Babylonian art. The gems and cylinders were for the most part intended to be used as seals, and some of them are provided with handles cut out of the stone, the seal itself having designs on four, and sometimes on five faces. These handles seem to be a peculiarity of Hittite art, or at least of the art which derived its inspiration from that of the Hittites. Another peculiarity noticeable in many of the gems, consists in enclosing the inner field of the engraved design with one or more concentric circles, each circle containing an elaborate series of ornaments or figures, or even characters, though the characters are usually placed in the central field. Thus two gems have been found at Yuzghât, in Kappadokia, so much alike, that they must have been the work of the same artist. On the larger an inscription has been engraved in the centre, round which runs a circle containing a large number of beautifully-executed figures. The winged solar disk rests upon the symbol of " kingship," on either side of which kneels a figure, half man and half bull. On the right and left is the figure of a standing priest, behind whom we see on the left a man adoring what seems to be the stump of a tree, while on the right are a tree, two arrows and a quiver, a basket, a stag's head, and a seated deity, above whose hand is a bird. The two groups are separated by the picture of a boot—the symbol, it may be, of the earth—which rests, like the winged solar disk, on the symbol of royalty. The smaller seal has a different inscription in the centre, encircled by two rings, one containing a row of ornaments, and the other the same figures as those engraved on the larger seal, excepting only that the arrangement of the figures has been changed, and a tree introduced among them. What is curious, however, is that a gem has been found at Aidin, far away towards the western extremity of Asia Minor, containing a central inscription almost identical with that of the smaller Yuzghât seal, though the figures which surround it are not the same.

These circular seals must be regarded not only as characteristic of Hittite art, but also as a product of Hittite invention. We meet with nothing resembling them in Babylonia or Assyria.

The gems can be traced across the Ægean to the shores of Greece. But the discoveries of Dr. Arthur Evans and Mr. Hogarth in Krete have shown that much that was once supposed to have been derived by Mykenæan art from Asia Minor may have developed independently among the cultured artists of the Mykenæan age. At the same time their fondness for composite animal forms points to Asianic influence, like the animal's heads and the boots with upturned toes which we find on the seals and gems of the primitive Greek world. At any rate, among the objects discovered by Dr. Schliemann at Mykenæ, there is more than one which reminds us how, according to Greek story, the lords of Mykenæ came from Lydia. Allusion has already been made to the figures of the Hittite goddess and the doves that rested on the pinnacles of her temple ; another figure in thin gold gives us a likeness of the Hittite goddess seated on the cliff of Sipylos, as she appeared before rain and tempest had changed her into " the weeping Niobê." Perhaps, however, the most striking illustration of the westward migration of Hittite influence, is to be found in the famous lions which stand fronting each other, carved on stone, above the great gate of the ancient Peloponnesian city. The lions of Mykenæ have long been known as the oldest piece of sculpture in Europe, but the art which inspired it was of Asiatic origin. A similar bas-relief has been discovered at Kümbet, in Phrygia, in the near vicinity of Hittite monuments ; and we have just seen that the heraldic position in which the lions are represented was a peculiar feature of Hittite art.

Greek tradition affirmed that the rulers of

Mykenæ had come from Lydia, bringing with them the civilization and the treasures of Asia Minor. The tradition has been confirmed by modern research. While certain elements belonging to the prehistoric culture of Greece, as revealed at Mykenæ and elsewhere, were derived from Egypt and Phœnicia, there are others which point to Asia Minor as their source. And the culture of Asia Minor was Hittite. Mr. Gladstone, therefore, may be right in seeing the Hittites in the Keteians of Homer—that Homer who told of the legendary glories of Mykenæ and the Lydian dynasty which held it in possession. Even the buckle, with the help of which the prehistoric Greek fastened his cloak, has been shown by a German scholar to imply an arrangement of the dress such as we see represented on the Hittite monument of Ibreez.

For us of the modern world, therefore, the resurrection of the Hittite people from their long sleep of oblivion possesses a double interest. They appeal to us not alone because of the influence they once exercised on the fortunes of the Chosen People, not alone because a Hittite was the wife of David and the ancestress of Christ, but also on account of the debt which the civilization of our own Europe owes to them. Our culture is the inheritance we have received from ancient Greece, and the first beginnings of Greek culture were derived from the Hittite conquerors of Asia Minor. The Hittite warriors who still guard the Pass of Karabel, on the very threshold of Asia, are symbols of the position occupied by the race in the education of mankind. The Hittites carried the time-worn civilizations of Babylonia and Egypt to the furthest boundary of Asia, and there handed them over to the West in the grey dawn of European history. But they never passed the boundary themselves ; with the conquest of Lydia their mission was accomplished, the work that had been appointed them was fulfilled.

CHAPTER VII

THE HIEROGLYPHIC INSCRIPTIONS

WHEN the first edition of this book was published, the meaning of the Hittite hieroglyphic inscriptions was still a mystery. Beyond the interpretation of two or three characters the veil that covered them was still unlifted, or at most but a very small corner of it had been raised. Our knowledge of the people who used them was derived from other sources than the written records they themselves had left. It was based on archæology rather than on philology, though it was none the less certain on that account. The monumental inscriptions and papyri of Assyria and Egypt, the sculptured stones and gems found on Hittite sites, the rocks covered with their undeciphered hieroglyphs, and the references to the Hittites in the Old Testament, were the materials that had enabled us to reconstruct the history of a forgotten race and to build up afresh the fabric of a vanished empire. Like the monsters of the geological past which the palæontologist has succeeded in restoring, the Hittites, too, had risen as it were from the dead at the call of archæology.

But the Hittite inscriptions, scanty and undeciphered as they were, were not altogether useless. They served to connect together the scattered remains of Hittite dominion, and to prove that the peculiar art they accompany was of Hittite origin. It was the Hittite hieroglyphs at the side of the warrior in the Pass of Karabel, and of the seated goddess on Mount Sipylos, that proved these monuments to have been carved by Hittite hands. It was similarly inscriptions containing Hittite characters which allowed us to trace the march of Hittite armies along the highroads of Asia Minor, to show how all these roads centred in Kappadokia, and to feel sure that Hittite princes once reigned in the city of Hamath.

The Hittite texts are distinguished by two characteristics. In the older inscriptions the hieroglyphs are invariably carved in relief; it is only in the later texts that they are incised. Then secondly the lines read alternately from right to left and from left to right, the direction towards which the characters look determining that in which they should be read. This alternate or *boustrophedon* mode of writing also characterizes early Greek inscriptions, and since it was not adopted by either Phœnicians, Kretans, Egyptians or Assyrians, the question arises whether the Greeks did not learn to write in such a fashion from neighbours who made use of the Hittite script.

Another characteristic of Hittite writing is the frequent employment of the heads of animals and men. It is very rarely that the whole body of an animal is drawn ; the head alone was considered sufficient. This peculiarity would of itself mark off the Hittite hieroglyphs from those of Egypt.

But a very short inspection of the characters is enough to make it clear that the Hittites could not have borrowed them from the Egyptians. The two forms of writing are utterly and entirely distinct. One of the most common of Hittite characters represents the snow-shoe, which, as we have seen, points to the northern ancestry of the Hittite tribes, while the ideograph which denotes a " country " is a picture of the mountain peaks of the Kappadokian plateau. Like the animals whose heads or forms are used as hieroglyphs, they indicate that the Hittite system of writing originated in Kappadokia, and not in the southern regions of Syria or Canaan.

THE BILINGUAL BOSS OF TARKONDEMOS.

THE LION OF MERASH.

It is probable, however, that the invention took place after the contact of the Hittites with Egypt, and their consequent acquaintance with the Egyptian form of script. Similar occurrences have happened in modern times. A Cheroki Indian in North America, who had seen the books of the white man, was led thereby to devise an elaborate mode of writing for his own countrymen, and the curious syllabary invented for the Vei negroes by one of their tribe had the same origin. So, too, we may imagine that the sight of the hieroglyphs of Egypt, and the knowledge that thoughts could be conveyed by them, suggested to some Hittite genius the idea of inventing a similar means of intercommunication for his own people. The gold of Asia Minor was exported to Egypt as far back as the days of the Sixth Dynasty, and an African negro was sent by the Hittite king to Thothmes III.

Like the Egyptian hieroglyphs the Hittite characters are used, sometimes as ideographs to express ideas, sometimes phonetically to represent syllables and letters, sometimes as determinatives to denote the class to which the word belongs to which they are attached. It would seem, moreover, that a word or syllable might be expressed by

multiplying the characters which denoted the
whole or part of it, just as was the case in Egyptian
writing in the age of Ramses II. At the same time
the number of separate characters found in the
Hittite inscriptions is far less than that employed
by the Egyptian scribes. At present not 200 are
known to exist, though almost every fresh inscription adds to the list. This comparative scarcity of
characters is due to the fact that as a rule it is only
the suffixes that are expressed phonetically, the
roots or stems of the words being denoted by
ideographs. It is but seldom that the latter are
written phonetically or that the ideographs denoting them are accompanied by their phonetic
equivalents.

We may gather that the oldest writing-material
of the Hittites consisted of plates of metal, on the
surface of which the characters were hammered
out from behind. The seal of the Hittite copy of
the treaty with Ramses II must have been engraved
in this manner, though both the obverse and the
reverse were beaten into relief. In the centre of
the obverse was a representation of the god Sutekh
embracing the Hittite king, while a line of hieroglyphs ran round him. This central ornamentation surrounded by a circular band of characters

or figures, was in accordance with the usual style of Hittite art, and we have many seals that illustrate it. The Egyptian monuments show us what the silver plate was like. It was of rectangular shape, with a ring at the top by which it could be suspended from the wall. Portions of the Hittite version of the treaty, in cuneiform characters and the Babylonian language, which was at that time the language of diplomacy, have been discovered at Boghaz Keui.

We knew that the Hittites in the age of the Exodus were already a literary people. The Egyptian records make mention of a certain Khalipasil, whose name is derived from that of Khalip or Aleppo, and describe him as " a writer of books of the vile Hittites." Like the Egyptian Pharaoh, the Hittite monarch was accompanied to battle by his scribes. The broken cuneiform tablets found on the site of the citadel at Boghaz Keui have shown that here too were two libraries similar to those that existed in the towns of Babylonia and Assyria.

These tablets, which were first noticed by M. Chantre, reveal to us the Hittite language of Kappadokia. The language is the same, or very nearly the same, as that of the two letters from

Arzawa which form part of the Tel el-Amarna correspondence, and to which reference has already been made. The tablets include documents written in the Assyrian language, which was at the time the language of diplomacy ; others are in three different languages spoken by the neighbours of the Hittites ; but by far the larger number are in the official Hittite of Boghaz Keui itself. Amongst the latter are bilingual texts in Hittite and Assyrian, as well as comparative dictionaries in which Hittite words are given with their equivalents in Assyrian and Sumerian. All this, with the help of the ideographs which are very numerous in the religious texts, has enabled us to decipher the language and compile its grammar and vocabulary. A Hittite cuneiform inscription can now be translated with certainty to a very large extent. But along with our new knowledge has come also the further knowledge that the language of the hieroglyphic inscriptions was not the same as that of Boghaz Keui, Khattusas, " the Hittite City," as it was called. Nor did it belong to the same period of history. The Hittite empire of Khattusas was destroyed about B.C. 1200 by invaders from the north, amongst whom Meshech, the Muskâ of the Assyrian monuments and the Moschians of classical geography, were the most prominent. On its ruins a second Hittite empire was founded by the Moschians, called Cilician by the Latin writer Solinus, the chief centre of which was at Tyana. It was the Moscho-Hittites who have left us most, if not all, of the hieroglyphic texts.

In these, more than twenty years ago, I pointed out that the figure of a yoke denoted the suffix of the nominative, and that as the Egyptian and Assyrian inscriptions showed that this case usually terminated in -s, the phonetic value of the hiero-glyph was probably -s. I had already, at the outset of my Hittite studies, discovered the determinative of " deity," which we now know to be probably a picture of a sacred stone wrapped in cloths, and this had led me to identify the curious symbol which at Ibreez in Cilicia accompanies the figure of the god Sandes or Tarkus, and must therefore represent his name. But it was just after my Paper was read in 1880 before the Society of Biblical Archæology, announcing the discovery of a Hittite empire and the connexion of the art of Asia Minor with that of Carchemish, that I fell across what I hoped would be the " Rosetta Stone " of Hittite decipherment. It was a bilingual inscription in cuneiform and Hittite, and was engraved on a disk or seal of silver.

The story of the seal is a strange one. It was purchased many years ago at Smyrna by M. Alexander Jovanoff, a well-known numismastist of Constantinople, who showed it to the Oriental scholar Dr. A. D. Mordtmann. Dr. Mordtmann made a copy of it, and found it to be a round silver plate, probably the pommel of a dirk, round the rim of which ran a cuneiform text. Within, occupying the central field, was the figure of a warrior in a new and unknown style of art. He stood erect, holding a spear in the right hand, and pressing the left against his breast. He was clothed in a tunic, over which a fringed cloak was thrown ; a close-fitting cap was on the head and boots with upturned ends on the feet, the upper part of the legs being bare, while a dirk was fastened in the belt. On either side of the figure was a series of " symbols," the series on each side being the same, except that on the right side the upper " symbols " were smaller and the lower " symbols " larger than the corresponding ones on the left side.

In an article published some years later on the cuneiform inscriptions of Van, Dr. Mordtmann referred to the seal, and it was his description of the figure in the centre of it which arrested my attention. I saw at once that the figure must be in the style of art I had just determined to be Hittite, and I guessed that the " symbols " which accompanied it would turn out to be Hittite hieroglyphs. Dr. Mordtmann stated that he had given a copy of the seal in 1862 in the " Numismatic Journal which appears in Hanover." After a long and troublesome search I found that the publication meant by him was not a Journal at all, and had appeared at Leipzig, not at Hanover, in 1863, not in 1862. The copy of the seal contained in it proved that I was right in believing Dr. Mordtmann's " symbols " to be Hittite characters.

It now became necessary to know how far the copy was correct, and to ascertain whether the original were still in existence. A reply soon came from the British Museum. The seal had once been offered to the Museum for sale, but rejected, as nothing like it had ever been seen before, and it was therefore suspected of being a forgery. Before its rejection, however, an electrotype had been taken of it, an impression of which was now sent to me.

Shortly afterwards came another communication

from M. François Lenormant, one of the most brilliant and learned Oriental scholars of the past century. He had seen the original at Constantinople some twenty years previously, and had there made a cast of it, which he forwarded to me. The cast and the electrotype agreed exactly together.

There could, accordingly, be no doubt that we had before us, if not the original itself, a perfect facsimile of it. The importance of this fact soon became manifest, for the original seal disappeared after M. Jovanoff's death, and in spite of all inquiries no trace of it could be discovered. I have just learnt, however, that it is said to have been found in a private collection in England.

The reading of the cuneiform legend has been the subject of much discussion, for the most part needless. It gives us the name of the king whose figure is engraved within it, and the first portion of it reads : " Tarqu-dimme king of the land." The second portion is of more doubtful interpretation, and the actual meaning of it could not have been arrived at with certainty before the decipherment of the Hittite texts. The last word *me-e* or *mê* is, in fact, a transliteration of the Hittite *mê* " I (am)," and the preceding character is not phonetic but the ideograph of " city." The whole legend is, consequently, " Tarqu-dimme king of the land of the city (am) I."

The name Tarqu-dimme is evidently the same as that of the Cilician prince Tarkondêmos or Tarkondimotos, who lived in the time of our Lord. The name is also met with in other parts of Asia Minor under the forms of Tarkondas and Tarkondimatos ; and we may consider it to be of a distinctly Hittite type. The seal probably came from Cilicia.

The twice-repeated Hittite version of the cuneiform legend naturally corresponds with the latter. But the arrangement of the characters composing it, due more to the necessity of filling up the vacant space on the seal than to the requirements of their natural order, allowed more than one interpretation of them. There were, however, two facts which furnished the key to their true reading. On the one hand, the inscription is divided into two halves by two characters whose form and position in other Hittite texts show them to signify " king " and " country " ; on the other hand, the first two characters are made, as it were, to issue from the mouth of the king, and must thus express his name. Hence the first of them, which represents the head of a goat, will have the ideographic value

of *tarqu*, while the second, which had not hitherto
been met with elsewhere in the inscriptions, will
be *dimme*. Then follow the ideographs of " king,"
" country," and " city," the first being a picture
of the royal and priestly tiara and the third a representation of a plough, while in the second Mordtmann had already seen a likeness of the peculiar
shafts of rock which rise out of the Kappadokian
plateau. The last character is phonetic, with the
value of *me*, a short oblique line attached to it
further expressing the vowel *e* of the cuneiform
text.

The hope I had cherished that in the bilingual
seal of Tarkondêmos we had found the key to
Hittite decipherment was not realized. The key
refused to turn in the lock. System after system
of decipherment was proposed, which satisfied
none but its author, and not always even him. For
more than twenty years I had vainly tried every
possible or impossible combination ; a blank wall
invariably defied my efforts. I came at last to the
conclusion that without a long bilingual inscription
the decipherment of the Hittite hieroglyphs was a
hopeless task.

For this the silver seal was itself in part re-
sponsible. It misled instead of assisting. The

analysis of the Hittite legend upon it given above
has been made possible only now that the decipherment of the texts has become an accomplished fact.
We now know that the last character but one is an
ideograph and not phonetic, and that the first
element in the name of the king is used with its
ideographic and not its usual phonetic value. This
was *is ;* it was only when it denoted a goat that it
was pronounced *tarqu.*

But it was not alone our misunderstanding of
the legend on the boss that stood in the way of a
successful decipherment of the inscriptions. The
inscriptions themselves were mainly in fault ; not
only were they few and mutilated, the copies we
possessed of them were bad and untrustworthy.
It is impossible to copy correctly half-obliterated
texts when we know neither the language nor the
true forms of the characters ; and this is especially
the case where the texts are in relief. The decipherer had to work with imperfect tools.

During the past twenty years, however, the
number of inscriptions has been considerably increased ; more perfect ones have been discovered ;
and above all we are no longer dependent on copies
made hastily with the eye and hand. When the
originals are not in the safe custody of a museum,

we now have casts, squeezes and photographs which reproduce them with fidelity, and can be examined and re-examined at leisure. We can now separate characters which had been confounded together, or trace the exact forms of misdrawn hieroglyphs.

The first result of this better acquaintance with the real forms of the Hittite characters was to reveal to me an important fact. In the early days of my Hittite studies, misled by the copies we then possessed of the Hamath texts, I had confused together the two ideographs of " king " and " district." Decipherer after decipherer had followed me in my error, thus missing the sense of the inscriptions and losing the help of the geographical key. As long as the ideograph of " district " was supposed to mean " king," the decipherer did not know where to look for the geographical names. Once the determinative was discovered, however, he knew that he would find them in the words to which it was attached.

The ideograph denoting a " district " which derived its name from the capital city is not quite the same as the ideograph for " country " which figures on the silver seal. It represents only one mountain peak, whereas the ideograph for " country " represents two. But the two ideographs interchange in the inscriptions, their signification being almost the same. There was yet a third ideograph with three peaks which was sometimes used in place of them, and properly signified a " mountainous land."

The discovery of the determinative of " district," or rather its separation from the ideograph of " king," gave me the clue for which I had so long been seeking. I could now tell where the geographical names in an inscription were to be found. And the first to be found was the name of Carchemish.

The name is met with in all the more perfect inscriptions of Jerablûs, and, with one exception, in them only. It stands at the head of the more complete texts and occupies the foremost place in the titles of the Carchemishian kings. It is, moreover, the only name to which the determinative of " district " is attached, so what it represents can no longer admit of doubt.

Many years ago the Dutch numismatist, M. Six, suggested to me that it was the name of Carchemish. I do not know what reasons he had for his suggestion, but the erroneous belief that the determinative of " district " was identical with the ideograph of " king " stood in the way of my accepting it, as well as the fact that the fourth character of which the name is composed is the goat's head. The seal of Tarkondêmos seemed to demand for the latter the sound of *tarqu*.

Since the death of M. Six, however, new inscriptions have come to light which show that the last argument cannot be pressed. In them the goat's head interchanges with the yoke when used to denote the suffix of the nominative, and it must therefore have the value of (*i*)*s*. It was only when signifying a " goat " that the hieroglyph was pronounced *tarqu*.

The name in which Six proposed to see that of Carchemish consists of four characters. The fourth and last, as I have said, is the goat's head. The third is the character which, as the bilingual seal has informed us, has the value of *me*. The second is a quiver for arrows, while the first is a hieroglyph which does not occur elsewhere in the inscriptions, and may accordingly be presumed to denote a closed, and not an open, syllable.

Now the quiver is frequently met with. It is found, for example, in a word which the ideograph often prefixed to it shows must mean " high-priest," and which, as we now know, was pronounced *kuanis*. As it represents the first syllable of the word, I had already therefore assigned to the quiver the value of *ka*.

Here, then, we have a territorial name, standing in the forefront of the inscriptions of Carchemish and practically unknown elsewhere, which consists of four characters, the last three of which represent the syllables *ka*, *me*, and *is*. That the first stands for *kar* is an irresistible conclusion. The decipherment of the Hittite texts has at last become possible !

The name of Carchemish also appears under an adjectival form agreeing with the substantive which precedes it. For reasons which need not be detailed here, I was able to show that the adjective should be read *Karkamêsiyas*, thus furnishing us with the values of three more characters *si*, *ya*, and *yas*. In one instance between *me* and *si* a character is inserted, which we find elsewhere inserted or omitted at will by the scribes. As was perceived by M. Halévy, it must therefore be a vowel, and its position in the name of Carchemish further indicates that it represents the vowel *i* or *e*. On similar grounds I was able to point out another vowel and to identify it with *a*.

Then came further discoveries. One of the

cases of the noun is denoted by the picture of a sleeve, and from its position in an inscription which runs round a bowl we gather that the case in question was the accusative. The same hieroglyph also denotes the ordinary suffix of the gentilic adjective, and what this was we have learned from geographical names preserved in Assyrian or classical texts, as well as from the name of Khattinâ applied by the Assyrians to the " Hittites " in the neighbourhood of the Orontes. The sleeve must therefore have the value of *n*, and the Hittite language, like that of Arzawa and Boghaz Keui, will have formed the nominative of the noun in *-s* and the accusative in *-n*, while the common suffix of the gentilic adjective was *-na(s)*.

Two other hieroglyphs interchange with the sleeve, and will accordingly have substantially the same pronunciation. Similarly we obtain for other characters the values of *-nas*, *-nis*, and *-nen*, while the interchange of other characters again with *me* and *s* enables us to discover the representatives of *ma*, *mes*, *as*, *iz*, and the like. In this way a sufficient number of values can be determined to form the beginnings of a working syllabary.

This we can now apply to an inscription from the site of the ancient Tyana, one of the few perfectly preserved texts which we possess. It begins with the name of the priest-king, followed by a gentilic adjective, to which the determinative of " district " is attached. This is composed of six characters, the last five of which I had read *a-n-a-na-s*. As *-nas* is the gentilic suffix, the name of the city will have ended in *-ana*, and the first character must consequently be *tu*.

But the phonetic decipherment of the inscriptions by no means exhausts our task. The texts are largely made up of ideographs ; in fact, as has already been stated, it is, as a general rule, only the grammatical suffixes and proper names that are expressed phonetically. Although, however, we cannot read the ideographs phonetically, we can in a considerable number of cases tell what they mean, thanks to their pictorial forms. As in all hieroglyphic systems of writing, plentiful use is made of determinatives, that is, of characters which indicate what is the class of words to which they are attached. Thus there are determinatives of priests and officials, of action and power.

Among the determinatives is one which is employed to divide words. Its meaning was discovered by Dr. Peiser, and it characterizes more especially the later inscriptions which are incised and not in relief. In the older texts it is found but rarely ; in these, indeed, it is prefixed only to words that denote officials. It serves to mark them off as a class apart, and so starts on its career as a " word-divider." Its importance to the decipherer need not be pointed out, for it tells him where words begin and where they end.

A commencement has thus been made in Hittite decipherment. But it must be remembered that it is a commencement only. There are many characters the phonetic values of which are merely probable or possible, there are many more to whose pronounciation there is as yet no clue. There are determinatives whose meanings have yet to be fixed, and ideographs whose signification is unknown. Our materials are still scanty and defective ; we need more inscriptions and, above all, more perfectly preserved inscriptions, before further progress is possible. Because I can partially read the few we possess, it would be affectation to pretend that I have any real knowledge of them. The names of the deities they mention are still undetermined ; even the royal names they contain can be read only in part.

Nevertheless, I can now make out the general

sense of most of the longer inscriptions, and draw certain historical conclusions from their contents. The three shorter Hamath texts, for instance, record the building or restoration of a temple which had been destroyed by an invader from the far north. The longer inscriptions of Carchemish do not belong to the same king. In one we read of the shrine and images that had been erected in the holy city of Carchemish ; another is merely a long list of the titles of the priest-king, while a third describes the appointment of various priests and the rededication of the sacred stone. But the most interesting fact connected with the inscriptions of Carchemish is derived from two half-obliterated texts cut on the rocks of Gurun in Eastern Kappadokia, where they were discovered by Sir Charles Wilson. Gurun lies on the banks of the Tokhma-Su, and is mentioned by Sennacherib under the name of Guriania, in a letter written to his father while he was still crown prince. The inscriptions are dedicated to the divine triad of Hittite religion, and record the name of a king of Carchemish who had carried his arms thus far. It is these inscriptions, which are duplicates one of the other, that form the sole exception to the exclusive occurrence of the name of Carchemish in the inscriptions of

Jerablûs. The whole country, however, from Malatiyeh southwards to Carchemish, must once have acknowledged the sway of the same Hittite king. This is clear from the fact that the lands which the king of Malatiyeh is said to govern are the same as those which are found in the titles of the kings at Carchemish. At what date this was the case we are still ignorant.

The Cilician inscriptions belong to a later epoch. Near the silver mines of Bulgar Maden a memorial of himself has been left by the high-priest Sandêtis, who calls himself *Sandanyas*, " the Sandanian," that is to say, " of the city of Sandes." This was the neighbouring town of Kybistra, known to the Greeks as Herakleia, the city of Hêraklês, who was identified by them with the Cilician god. It is still termed Eregli. Sandêtis further declares that he belonged to the family of King Eminias, whose image is found sculptured on the rock at Ivriz, westward of Bulgar Maden. On a stela found at Bor, the ancient Tyana, are also the portrait and written record of the king. My translation of his inscription would be as follows : " Eminias, the Tyanian priest-king, the dirk-bearer, the lordly, the prince of Cilicia, the priest, the lord of the men of the city of the Eneti. The sacred stone of Sandes (or Tarkus), king of this royal city of the Eneti, as it was of old, I dedicated and restored."

The kings are high-priests as well as kings, in accordance with the fact that the cities over which they ruled were sacred, being not only consecrated to a deity but themselves deities, and, as such, objects of worship.

It is possible that the Hittite system of writing did not pass away without leaving some permanent traces of its existence in the alphabets which superseded it. Apart from certain characters peculiar to the alphabets of Asia Minor, it may be that the names assigned to the letters even of the Phœnician alphabet were influenced by it. When the Phœnicians borrowed or adapted the alphabet called after them, they gave names to the letters beginning in their own language with the sounds expressed by the several symbols. Thus *a* was termed *aleph*, because the Phœnician word *aleph* began with that sound, *k* was *kaph*, " the hand," because *kaph* in Phœnician began with *k*. It was but an early application of the principle which made our forefathers believe that the child would learn his alphabet more quickly if he were taught that " *A* was an archer who shot at a frog."

But the names must have been assigned to the letters not only because they commenced with corresponding sounds, but also because of their fancied resemblance to the objects denoted by the names. Now in some instances the resemblance is by no means clear. The earlier forms of the letters called *kaph* and *yod*, for example, both of which words signify " a hand," have little likeness to the human hand. If we turn to the Hittite hieroglyphs, however, we find among them two representations of the hand, encased in the long Hittite glove, which are almost identical with the Phœnician letters in shape. It is difficult, therefore, to resist the conclusion that the letters *kaph* and *yod* received their names from Syrians who were familiar with the appearance of the Hittite characters. It is the same in the case of *aleph*. Here, too, the old Phœnician letter does not in any way resemble an ox, but it bears a close likeness to the head of a bull, which occupies a prominent position in the Hittite texts. *Aleph* became the Greek *alpha* when the Phœnician alphabet was handed on to the Greeks, and in the word *alphabet* has become part of our own heritage. Like *yod*, which has passed through the Greek *iota* into the English *jot*, it is thus possible that there are still words in daily use among ourselves which can be traced, if not to the Hittite language, at all events to the Hittite hieroglyphic script.

The Hittite languages were Asianic, that is to say, they belonged to a group peculiar to Asia Minor. Long ago the Hittite proper names preserved on the Egyptian and Assyrian monuments showed that Hittite was not Semitic ; but it was not until the discovery of the cuneiform tablets of Arzawa and Boghaz Keui that its exact character was disclosed. In many respects it resembled the Indo-European languages ; indeed, its grammatical and structural likeness to Greek is almost startling. But the same likeness is displayed by the language of the Lykian inscriptions, which will possibly turn out to be related to that of the Hittite tribes. As in Indo-European, so, too, in Hittite and Lykian the relations of grammar were expressed by suffixes.

Whether there is any connexion between Hittite and the languages of ancient Armenia and Mesopotamia, which have been revealed to us by the cuneiform texts of Van and Mitanni, is more problematical. But in all three we have the same linguistic type and a remarkable similarity of grammatical flexion. The nominative and accusative of the noun, for example, are in all alike denoted by the terminations -s and -n.

We must be on our guard, however, against supposing that there was but one uniform language throughout the district in which the Hittite population lived. Different tribes doubtless spoke different dialects, and some of these dialects probably differed a good deal from one another. But they all belonged to one and the same form of speech, and may therefore be collectively spoken of as the Hittite language, just as the various dialects of England are collectively termed English. Indeed, it is difficult to find any indications of dialectical differences in the existing hieroglyphic inscriptions, in whatever part of Asia Minor or Syria they are met with. They all exhibit the same suffixes and the same groups of characters constituting words.

The Hittites of Southern Palestine must have lost their old language and have adopted that of their Semitic neighbours at an early period. In Northern Syria the change was longer in coming about. The last king of Carchemish bears a non-Semitic name, but a Semitic god was worshipped at Aleppo, and Kadash on the Orontes remained a Semitic sanctuary. The Hittite occupation of

Hamath seems to have lasted for a short time only. The king who appears on the Assyrian monuments as the contemporary of Ahab has the Semitic name of Irkhulena, " the moon is our god " ; and his successors were equally of Semitic origin. It is more doubtful whether Tou or Toi, whose son came to David with an offer of alliance, bears a name which can be explained from the Semitic lexicon.

In the fastnesses of the Taurus, however, the Hittite dialects were slow in dying. In the days of St. Paul the people of Lystra still spoke " the speech of Lycaonia," although the official language of Kappadokia had long before become Aramaic. But the Aramaic was itself supplanted by Greek, and before the downfall of the Roman empire Greek was the common language of all Asia Minor. In its turn Greek has had to make way in these modern times for Turkish.

Languages, however, may change and perish, but the races that have spoken them remain. The characteristics of race, once acquired, are slow to alter. Though the last echoes of Hittite speech have died away centuries ago, the Hittite race still inhabits the region from which in ancient days it poured down upon the cities of the south.

We may still see in it all the lineaments of the warriors of Karabel or the sculptured princes of Carchemish ; even the snow-shoe and fingerless glove are still worn on the cold uplands of Kappadokia.

CHAPTER VIII

HITTITE TRADE AND INDUSTRY

THE Hittites shone as much in the arts of peace as in the arts of war. The very fact that they invented a system of writing speaks highly for their intellectual capacities. It has been granted to but few among the races of mankind to devise means of communicating their thoughts otherwise than by words ; most of the nations of the world have been content to borrow from others not only the written characters they use but even the conception of writing itself.

We know from the ruins of Boghaz Keui and Eyuk that the Hittites were no mean architects. They understood thoroughly the art of fortification ; the great moat outside the walls of Boghaz Keui, with its sides of slippery stone, is a masterpiece in this respect, like the fortified citadels within the city, to which the besieged could retire when the outer wall was captured. The well-cut blocks and sculptured slabs of which their palaces were built prove how well they knew the art of quarrying and fashioning stone. The mines of the Bulgar Dagh are an equally clear indication of their skill in mining and metallurgic work.

The metallurgic fame of the Khalybes, who bordered on the Hittite territory, and may have belonged to the same race, was spread through the Greek world. They had the reputation of first discovering how to harden iron into steel. It was from them, at all events, that the Greeks acquired the art.

Silver and copper appear, from the evidence of the Egyptian and Assyrian monuments, to have been the metals most in request, though gold and iron also figure among the objects which the Hittites offered in tribute. The gold and copper were moulded into cups and images of animals, and the copper was changed into bronze by being mixed with tin. From whence the tin was procured we have yet to learn.

Silver and iron were alike used as a medium of exchange. The Assyrian king received from Carchemish 250 talents of iron ; and the excavations of Dr. Schliemann among the ruins of Troy have afforded evidence that silver also was employed by the Hittites in place of money, and that its use for this purpose was communicated by them to the most distant nations of Western Asia Minor.

In the co-called " treasure of Priam," disinterred among the calcined ruins of Hissarlik or Troy, are six blade-like ingots of silver, about seven or eight inches in length and two in breadth. Mr. Barclay Head has pointed out that each of these ingots weighs the third part of a Babylonian maneh or mina, and further that this particular maneh of 8,656 grains Troy, was once employed throughout Asia Minor for weighing bullion silver. It differed from the standard of weight and value used in Phœnicia, Assyria, and Asia Minor itself in the later Greek age. But it corresponded with " the maneh of Carchemish " mentioned in the Assyrian contract tablets, which continued to hold its own even after the conquest of Carchemish by Sargon. The maneh of Carchemish had, it is true, been originally derived from Babylonia, like most of the elements of Hittite culture, but it had made itself so thoroughly at home in the Hittite capital as to be called after its name. Nothing can show more clearly than this the leading position held by the Hittites in general, and the city of Carchemish in particular, in regard to commerce and industry.

Carchemish was, in fact, the centre of the over-land trade in Western Asia. It commanded the high-road which brought the products of Phœnicia and the West to the civilized populations of Assyria and Babylon. It was this which made its posses-sion so greatly coveted by the Assyrian kings. Its capture assured to Sargon the command of the Mediterranean coast, and the transference to Assyrian hands of the commerce and wealth which had flowed in to the merchant-princes of the Hittite city.

The sumptuous furniture in which they indulged is mentioned by Assur-natsir-pal. Like the luxurious monarchs of Israel, they reclined on couches inlaid with ivory, of which it is possible that they were the inventors. At all events, elephants were still hunted by Tiglath-pileser I in the neighbourhood of Carchemish, as they had been by Thothmes III four centuries earlier, and elephants' tusks were among the tribute paid by the Hittites to the Assyrian kings. It may be that the extinction of the elephant in this part of Asia was due to Hittite huntsmen.

The ivory couches of Carchemish, however, were not employed at meals, as they would have been in Assyria or among the Greeks and Romans of a later day. Like the Egyptians, the Hittites sat when eating, and their chairs were provided with backs as well as with curiously-formed footstools. The food was placed on low cross-legged tables which resembled a camp-stool in shape.

At times, as we may gather from a bas-relief at Merash, they entertained themselves at a banquet with the sounds of music. Several different kinds of musical instruments are represented on the monuments, among which we may recognize a lyre, a trumpet, and a sort of guitar. It is evident that they were fond of music, and had cultivated the art, as befitted a people to whom wealth had given leisure. A curious indication of the same leisured ease is to be found in a sculpture at Eyuk, where an attendant is depicted carrying a monkey on his shoulders. Those only who enjoyed the quiet of a peaceful and wealthy life would have gratified the taste for animals which the monuments reveal, by importing an animal like the monkey from the distant south. The Hittites were doubtless a warlike people when they first swooped down upon the plains of Syria, but they soon began to cultivate the arts of peace and to become one of the great mercantile peoples of the ancient world.

We learn from the Book of Kings that horses and chariots were exported from Egypt for the Hittite princes, the Israelites serving as intermediaries in the trade. But they must also have obtained horses from the north, and perhaps have bred them for themselves. The prophet Ezekiel tells us (xxvii. 14) that " they of Togarmah traded " in the fairs of Tyre " with horses and horsemen and mules," and Togarmah has been identified with the Til-Garimmi of the Assyrian inscriptions, which was situated north of Harran. In the wars between Egypt and Kadesh a portion of the Hittite army fought in chariots, each drawn by two horses, and holding sometimes two, sometimes three men. The chariots were of light make, and rested on two wheels, usually furnished with six spokes.

The army was well disciplined and well arranged. Its nucleus was formed of native-born Hittites, who occupied the centre and the posts of danger. Around them were ranged their allies and mercenaries, under the command of special generals. The native infantry and cavalry also obeyed separate captains, but the whole host was led by a single commander-in-chief.

We have yet to be made acquainted with the details of their domestic architecture. The ground-plan of their palaces has been given us at Boghaz Keui and Eyuk, at Carchemish and Zinjerli, and we know that they were built round a central court of quadrangular form. We know, too, that the entrance to the palace was, like that to an Egyptian temple, flanked by massive blocks of stone on either side, and approached by an avenue of sculptured slabs. We have learned, moreover, that the palace was erected on raised terraces or mounds ; but beyond this we know little except that use was made of a pillar without a base, which had been originally derived from Babylonia, the primitive home of columnar architecture.

About the Hittite dress we have fuller information. Apart from the snow-shoes or moccasins which have helped to identify their monumental remains, we have found the Hittites wearing on their heads two kinds of covering, one a close-fitting skull-cap, the other a lofty tiara, generally pointed, but sometimes rounded at the top or ornamented, as at Ibreez, with horn-like ribbons. The pointed tiara was adorned with perpendicular lines of embroidery. At Boghaz Keui the goddesses have what has been termed the mural crown, resembling as it does the fortified wall of a town.

The robes of the women descended to the feet.

This was also the case with the long-sleeved gar-
ment of the priests, but other men wore a tunic
which left the knees bare, and was fastened round
the waist by a girdle. Over this was thrown a
cloak, which in walking left one leg exposed. In
the girdle was stuck a short dirk ; the other arms
carried being a spear and a bow, which was slung
behind the back. The double-headed battle-axe
was also a distinctively Hittite weapon, and was
carried by them to the coast of the Ægean, where
in the Greek age it became the symbol of the Karian
Zeus, and of the island of Tenedos. All these
weapons were of bronze, or perhaps of iron ; but
there are indications that the Hittite tribes had once
contented themselves with tools and weapons of
stone. Near the site of Arpad Mr. Boscawen purchased a large and beautiful axe-head of highly
polished green-stone, which could, however, never
have been intended for actual use. It was, in fact,
a sacrificial weapon, surviving in the service of the
gods from the days when the working of metal
was not yet known. Like other survivals in
religious worship, it bore witness to a social condition that had long since passed away. A small
axe-head, also of polished green-stone, was obtained
by myself from the neighbourhood of Ephesos,

and bears a remarkable resemblance in form to the axe-head of Arpad. The importance of this fact becomes manifest when we compare the numerous other weapons or implements of polished stone found in Western Asia Minor, which exhibit quite a different shape. It permits the conclusion that both Arpad and Ephesos had once submitted to the same influence, and that in both the same form of stone implement—a survival from an earlier age of stone—was dedicated to the service of the gods.

The dresses of cloth and linen with which the Hittites clothed themselves were dyed with various colours, and were ornamented with fringes and rich designs. That of the priest at Ibreez is especially worthy of study. Among the patterns with which it is adorned are the same square ornament as is met with on the tomb of the Phrygian king Midas, and the curious symbol usually known as the "swastika" which has become so famous since the excavations of General di Cesnola in Cyprus, and of Dr. Schliemann at Troy. The symbol recurs times without number on the prehistoric pottery of Cyprus and the Trojan plain; but no trace of it has ever yet been found in Egypt, in Assyria, or in Babylonia. Alone among the remains of the civilized nations of the ancient East the rock-sculpture of Ibreez displays it on the robe of a Lykaonian priest. Was it an invention of the Hittite people, communicated by them to the rude tribes of Asia Minor, along with the other elements of a cultured life, or was it of barbarous origin, adopted by the Hittites from the earlier population of the West ?

Before we can answer this question we must know far more than we do at present about that long-forgotten but wonderful race, whose restoration to history has been one of the most curious discoveries of the present age. When the sites of the old Hittite cities have been thoroughly explored, when the monuments they left behind them have been disinterred, and their inscriptions have been deciphered and read, we shall doubtless learn the answers to this and many other questions that are now pressing for solution. Meanwhile we must be content with what has already been gained. Light has been cast upon a dark page in the history of Western Asia, and therewith upon the sacred record of the Old Testament, and a people has advanced into the forefront of modern knowledge who exercised a deep influence upon the fortunes of Israel, though hitherto they had been to us little more than a name. At the very moment when every word of Scripture is being minutely scrutinized, now by friends, now by foes, we have learnt that the statement once supposed to impugn the authority of the sacred narrative is the best witness to its truth. The friends of Abraham, the allies of David, the mother of Solomon, all belonged to a race which left an indelible mark on the history of the world, though it has been reserved in God's wisdom for our own generation to discover and trace it out.

CHAPTER IX

THE DISCOVERIES AT BOGHAZ KEUI

THE last edition of this book was published in 1903. Three years later, in 1906–7, Boghaz Keui was partially excavated by the Germans under the superintendence of Dr. Winckler. Two libraries of cuneiform tablets, similar to the libraries of Babylonia and Assyria, were discovered, one on the eastern side of the great temple of the supreme god Tessub, the other on the western side of the ancient citadel, now called Böjuk-kala', as well as on the flat ground below it. The tablets found by the side of the temple are of black and grey clay, and thus distinguished from those found near the citadel which are yellow and brown in colour. The one belonged to a temple library, the others were probably a royal collection.

Unfortunately they were mostly broken. The rocky soil of Boghaz Keui was not so favourable to their preservation as the soft alluvial clay of Babylonia. But before the German excavations

were closed a vast number of fragments were disinterred from the ground. Many of them are in
the Museum at Constantinople ; more than 20,000
are in Berlin. In spite of the interruption caused
by the Great War, the work of examining, cleaning, uniting, copying and deciphering the tablets
has gone on apace, and a new world has come to
light. The earlier history of Asia Minor has been
opened up to us and the important part it played
in the development of culture has been made
manifest.

New light has also come from the records of
Babylonia, and the Hittites have taken their place
in ancient history by the side of the Babylonians
and Egyptians. It was with good reason that Heth
in the tenth chapter of Genesis is declared to have
been the second son of Canaan.

But we now know that the name Hittite was
applied to different peoples and languages. It
meant to the Babylonians the nations of eastern
Asia Minor who participated in a common culture,
and at one time, at any rate, acknowledged the
same government. On the racial side, however,
they were probably quite as much mixed as the
inhabitants of the British Isles, and just as different languages are spoken in Great Britain, so,

too, different languages were spoken among them. In the days of the first Hittite empire, which had its seat at Boghaz Keui, the language which may be termed official Hittite had many affinities to the Indo-European languages of Europe, and differed entirely from what has been called Proto-Hittite, since the latter was the original language of the founders of the Hittite dynasties, while the Moscho-Hittite language of the hieroglyphic texts differed again from both of them.

The Moscho-Hittites do not appear upon the scene until after B.C. 1200. They formed part of those " nations of the north," some of whom were Achæans and other ancestors of the later Greeks, who overthrew the earlier Hittite empire and attacked Egypt in the days of the Pharaoh Ramses III. The Moscho-Hittites established the second Hittite empire, termed Cilician by the Latin writer Solinus, and made Tyana, the modern Bor, the centre of their sovereignty, though Carchemish also occupied a dominant place.

The British Museum excavations at Carchemish in 1911–14 and 1920, under Dr. Hogarth and Mr. Woolley, have cleared up the earlier history of that city. In pre-Hittite days it shared the culture of Northern Syria, which seems to have had its

roots in Sumerian Babylonia and Elam, and at one
time was under the rule of kings who governed
the Semitic territory of Khana or Mari to the
south of it. Then came its occupation by the
Hittites about 1900 B.C. Mursilis I, the Hittite
king, marched against Babylon ; the dynasty of
Amraphel was overthrown, and northern Syria
fell into the hands of the invaders from Asia
Minor. From this time forward Carchemish
became the south-eastern outpost of the Hittite
monarchs. It commanded the ford across the
Euphrates and therewith the high-road of trade to
the cultured lands of the East. The names of
some of its vassal kings are found in the Hittite
texts and part of a letter from the Hittite sovereign
to one of them, Biyassilis by name, has been preserved. In this the king tells his correspondent
that the government of Carchemish is assigned to
him and his heirs for ever—that is to say as long
as they continued to be faithful to their overlord.
Biyassilis took part in the wars of the Hittite
monarch Subbi-luliuma against Mitanni or Mesopotamia, and in the treaty made by Subbi-luliuma
with his conquered foes it was expressly stipu-
lated that no hostile force should ever be sent
against Carchemish and that the rulers of Car-

chemish and Mitanni should remain united together in eternal " brotherhood."

When the first Hittite empire was destroyed Carchemish fell to the lot of the Moschians, and passed under the government of priest-kings or high-priests who owned allegiance to the king of Tyana, in Cilicia. It became, in fact, what the Greeks called a Hierapolis, or Holy City, dedicated to the water-goddess Nina, and its rulers, consequently, were high-priests rather than kings. Gradually, however, its dependence upon Cilicia weakened, it grew rich through trade, and the second Hittite empire broke up into independent fragments. When the Assyrians attacked the city and it was eventually captured by them in 717 B.C., it was an independent state.

The Hittites first make their appearance in history in the age of Sargon of Akkad, about 2700 B.C. The story of an expedition of the Babylonian king, written in what may be called Hittite-Babylonian, has been found among the ruins of the house of the Hittite ambassador at Tel el-Amarna, in Egypt. The expedition is represented as having been of a botanical rather than a military character ; at all events its chief object and result seem to have been the transportation of the pomegranate, the vine and the rose to Babylonia—which doubtless expressed a historical fact. The "mountain" of Barsukhanda, not far to the north of the Gulf of Antioch, was the furthest point that was reached. Naram-Sin, the grandson of Sargon, made a much more ambitious attempt, a fragmentary account of which, in the Hittite language, has been discovered at Boghaz Keui. An alliance against the Babylonian monarch had been formed between the nations of the north-east, which included Barsukhanda, Garsaura on the Halys, Kanes (near Kaisariyeh), the Mitannian Amorites, and Pamba, "king of the Hittites." Three campaigns were needed before the confederacy could be overthrown and the allies compelled to sue for peace and send tribute to Akkad.

The Semitic Assyrians were already established in Asia Minor. The king of Barsukhanda bears a Semitic name, and the city of Kanes mentioned above, and now represented by the great mounds of Kara Eyuk, was an important centre of trade. The copper, lead and silver mines of the Taurus were worked by Babylonian firms whose agents made Kanes their residence. A large part of the copper and most of the silver used in the ancient world at the time came from thence. The Hittites were already in touch with the civilisation and culture of Babylonia.

A little later, about 2300 B.C., Kanes was at the height of its prosperity. There were roads throughout the country along which consignments of metals were transported, and postmen carried letters and money orders written, not on paper, but on clay. But, it would appear, the native states still regarded the Babylonians and Assyrians with suspicion, if not with hostility, and so had not as yet accepted the Babylonian system of education and script. That came subsequently, after the destruction of Kanes, in the time of Khammurabi or Amraphel. Then it was that the literary culture of Babylonia was adopted as completely and whole-heartedly as Chinese and, in our own days, European culture have been adopted by the Japanese.

Meanwhile the little Hittite state had been developing into an empire. Its earlier rulers had been kings only of Kussar, probably the classical Garsaura, and it was not until they had established themselves at Boghaz Keui, on the eastern side of the Halys, that their power may be said to have really commenced. The city was called by them Khattusas or Khattusis, " the Hittite city," and we learn that the name also signified " Silver-town." We may therefore conclude that its rise was due to its becoming a seat of the silver trade. The power of the Hittite kings rested on the support of an army largely composed of men belonging to a different race. They had come from Thrace and the valley of the Danube, if we may trust the evidence of pottery and Greek tradition, and were the ancestors of the people subsequently known as Phrygians. The monarchy was established upon a feudal system ; the holders of property constituted the free population, who met in a general assembly and, under the presi-dency of the king, determined the laws and constitution of the country. They held their lands on condition of serving in the army when called upon to do so and of cultivating the fields assigned to them. Instead of military service, some of them were required to carry on certain trades like weaving, carpentry or metal work.

Besides the regular army the king had a body-guard, the members of which were known as Lulakhkhi and Khabiri. The Khabiri, of whom 1,200 were stationed in Boghaz Keui, derived both their institution and name from Babylonia, where we first hear of them in the time of Amraphel.

They were mercenary troops, and in later days played a conspicuous part in the Tel el-Amarna correspondence. In Babylonia they seem to have been mainly recruited from Elam ; in Asia Minor in the Greek period they came from Thrace.

The Hittite kings themselves, as their names show, belonged to the older population, which spoke a language known as Proto-Hittite. The examples of it in the Boghaz Keui cuneiform tablets are only partially deciphered ; the language itself is a very complicated one, unlike any other at present known, and the tablets containing Proto-Hittite texts with " official " Hittite translations attached to them are very few in number.

" Official " Hittite is a mixed language like English. It has borrowed largely from Assyrian, and still more largely from Indo-European. Indeed, so much has been borrowed from Indo-European in respect of grammar as well as vocabulary that some scholars have believed it to be Indo-European in origin, though mixed with non-Indo-European elements. But it is better to regard its basis as having been a language (or the dialect of a language) termed Luian or Luvian, specimens of which have been found in the Boghaz Keui tablets.

Boghaz Keui was the meeting place of merchants from all parts of the world, as well as the capital of an empire which had relations with both east and west. It is not surprising, therefore, that several different languages were represented in its libraries. Besides official Hittite, Proto-Hittite and Luian, there were Semitic Babylonian, the language of diplomacy, and consequently the language in which foreign treaties were . written, the old extinct Sumerian, which had become the Latin of the ancient world, and the language of the Mitannians of Mesopotamia. A treatise upon horse-breeding contains numerous words which are purely Sanskrit, the breeders and trainers of horses being a people who spoke Sanskrit and had not yet found their way to the north-west of India.

Labarnas, the grandfather of Mursilis I, was the founder of the first Hittite empire. He established himself at Khattusas (Boghaz Keui) and conquered the country as far as the Mediterranean. Mursilis, the son of Khattusilis I, made himself master of Aleppo and Northern Syria and captured Babylon, the spoil of which, we are told, he carried back to Asia Minor. Then came a period of palace revolts and murder on the part of the leaders of the

army, but eventually Telibinus I suppressed his
competitors and started a new dynasty. He restored Hittite rule in Syria and included Damascus
among his conquests. This would have been about
1700 B.C. Vassal kinglets were appointed at
Aleppo, Carchemish and Tegarama, the Togarmah
of the Old Testament, which lay to the north-west
of Harran.

Another dynasty appears to have arisen at
Khattusas under Dudkhaliyas II about 1430 B.C.
His grandson Subbi-luliuma carried the Hittite
arms far and wide. Syria was overrun ; its cities,
which had acknowledged the suzerainty of Egypt
throughout the preceding century and a half, were
forced to transfer their allegiance to the Hittite
king, and the chiefest among them, Kadesh on the
Orontes, became an unwilling ally of the northern
power. The Amorites, under their king, Ebed-
Asherah, and his son Aziru, followed its example.
Letters exist, indeed, in the Tel el-Amarna collection, in which the Amorite princes profess their
loyalty to the Egyptian government, but we now
know from the Boghaz Keui records that the
charges preferred against them at the Egyptian
court were founded on fact.

Meanwhile Subbi-luliuma was carrying on war

against an important ally of the Egyptians, Tusratta of Mitanni or Mesopotamia. But the
Mitannians proved to be no match for their
opponents ; Tusratta was defeated and subsequently murdered in a revolution at home, while
his kingdom was dismembered and placed under
Hittite control. Subbi-luliuma was now free to
annex the countries further north at the source
of the Euphrates, Alzu on the Arsanias being one
of them.

Large portions of western Asia Minor, more
especially on the Mediterranean coast, had long
been more or less subject to the Hittite power.
The " four kings " of Arzawa or western Cilicia,
like the Lycians (Lugga), acknowledged their
supremacy, and Hittite armies made their way,
sometimes to spoil and conquer, sometimes to give
help to their allies, as far as the Ægean. Mursilis
III, the son of Subbi-luliuma, who succeeded his
elder brother Arnuandas I on the throne, when
asked by the Lycians to assist them, carried his
arms as far as Taruisa or Troy and handed over
the government of a province to Tawagalawas, the
leader of the Akhkhiyawa or Achæans. These
latter had already appeared in Hittite history ;
Antaraus (the Greek Andreus), the father of

Tawagalawas, being described as king of the Achæans (Akhkhiyawa) and Lesbos (Lazpa).

Mursilis III had three sons and one daughter, the youngest of the sons being Khattusilis. The eldest son died before his father, who was accordingly succeeded by his second son, Muwatallis or Mutallis, " the Courageous." Khattusilis was still young, and was, moreover, weakly, and consequently had been adjudged unfit for military life and dedicated as a priest to the service of the goddess Istar. After his brother's accession, however, he seems to have recovered his strength ; he was made commander-in-chief of the army and, after suppressing disturbances in the north, defeated the Kaskians, who had invaded and occupied the eastern portion of the Hittite territory. In his brother's campaign against Ramses II of Egypt, to which reference is made in the treaty transcribed on a former page (p. 41), Khattusilis not only sent troops to Egypt, but also followed them himself. By this time he had become governor of the country north of Boghaz Keui, on the Paphlagonian frontier and the banks of the Iris, known as " Upper Asia," where he made the city of Khakwissa his capital and was invested by his brother with the title of " king."

Mutallis died soon after the Egyptian campaign, and his son Urkhi-Tessub, who succeeded him, soon quarrelled with his uncle. The result was civil war, and the capture of Urkhi-Tessub, who, after being imprisoned in the city of Samukha, " like a pig in his sty," was exiled into Syria. There he was accused of intriguing with the Babylonians, and was accordingly sent across the sea to Cyprus. As we hear no more of him, he was probably put to death there.

Meanwhile Khattusilis III had ascended the Hittite throne. He made peace with Egypt and became the ally of the Pharaoh. Portions of the Hittite text of the famous treaty between the two sovereigns have been found at Boghaz Keui. The language of it is not Hittite, but Babylonian, that being the diplomatic language of the time, as French is to-day, but while the Egyptian contains Babylonian idioms, the Babylonian (or Assyrian) version shows signs of Hittite influence. It would seem, therefore, that the treaty had been first written in Hittite and then translated into Babylonian and finally into Egyptian.

Khattusilis was wise in becoming the ally of Egypt. A formidable enemy in the shape of Assyria had arisen in the east which threatened alike Babylonia to the south of it and the Hittite and Egyptian possessions in Syria and Palestine. Mitanni (Mesopotamia) had become powerless and was, in fact, dependent upon Assyria, Babylonia was decadent, and the Amorite allies of the Hittites were weak and comparatively few in number. A coalition of the three leading powers of the ancient world was needed if the balance of power were to be preserved.

The reign of Khattusilis—whose name signifies " native of Khattusas " or Boghaz Keui—seems to have been a long one. He was followed on the throne by his son Dudkhaliyas III, whose name is identical with that of Tid'al, king of the (northern) nations, in the 14th chapter of Genesis. The Achæans now appear again upon the scene under a chieftain named Attarissiyas. He invaded the Hittite-protected states in south-west Asia Minor, and with a fleet of 100 vessels made a descent upon the Pamphylian coast. Though Dudkhaliyas claims to have defeated him, we find him once more attacking Hittite territory in the reign of Arnuwandas II, the son and successor of Dudkhaliyas. One of his raids was against Alasia, the Elishah of the Old Testament, which many scholars identify with Cyprus.

It was the beginning of that movement of " the peoples of the north " of which the Egyptian annals speak. Barbarian tribes from the Balkans, uniting with Achæan Greeks and the populations of the Black Sea, descended upon the civilised nations of the Oriental world. Arnuwandas was followed by his son Dudkhaliyas IV, and then the first Hittite empire and kingdom alike passed away. The city of Khattusas was captured and despoiled, the land of the Amorites was occupied by the pirates of the north and Egypt was saved only by a hair's breadth. The great battle fought on land and sea in the eighth year of Ramses III (1195 B.C.) prevented Egyptian civilisation from sharing the fate of that of Krete, of Mykenæ or of Khattusas.

But the Moschians who had followed in the wake of the barbaric torrent had participated in the old culture of the Hittites, and when the flood had passed southward they remained behind in eastern Asia Minor and a new Hittite empire and civilisation arose on the ruins of the old. Khattusas was again inhabited ; the rock-temple of Yasili-Kaya, with its sculptures, came into existence, and Tyana became the capital of an empire which extended once more eastward as far as Carchemish and even Melitênê. The story of this empire has been told in the preceding pages as well as that of the hieroglyphs which took the place of the cuneiform characters and may be regarded as the outward symbol of the new order of things.

But it is not only history which the tablets of Boghaz Keui are revealing to us. The geography and religion of early Asia Minor are also coming to light. Indeed by far the larger number of tablets relate to religion and ritual. Many of them are translations of Babylonian texts ; this is more particularly the case as regards the astrological and augural texts which seem to have made a special appeal to Hittite superstition. The ritual texts are multitudinous, like the ceremonies which they prescribe. As was natural among so mixed a population the deities they worshipped were very numerous ; temples and symbols of the gods stood on all sides ; there were priests of all ranks and degrees, and the rites and ceremonies they practised were extraordinarily elaborate.

Then, again, the Hittite libraries contained works by famous writers who flourished in various parts of Asia Minor, Arzawa or Cilicia, Kizzuwadna and Komana, and even Mitanni. Kikkuli, who wrote a work in several books on the breeding

and training of horses by the Sanskrit-speaking
Aryans of Mesopotamia and Asia Minor, was a
Mitannian, and another Mitannian, Kessê, translated the famous Babylonian Epic of Gilgames into
his own language. There was also a translation of
the poem into Hittite. The Hittites, however, had
their own poets and national or religious poems,
one of which was on the slaying of the Great
Serpent.

But perhaps the most interesting portion of
Hittite literature which has come down to us is the
Code of Laws. The Code, which goes back to the
earlier days of the Hittite Empire, was revised at
a later date, when many of the laws contained in it
were mitigated. In several instances, for example,
a fine was reduced by half or even remitted altogether, while the punishment of death ceased to
be inflicted except in certain extreme cases. In
its earlier form the Code contrasts favourably on
the side of humanity with those of other ancient
nations. It is less severe than the Babylonian
Code of Khammurabi or Amraphel, and far more
humane than that of the Assyrians, which, as might
be inferred from the character of the people, was
thoroughly Draconian. In all three Codes, however, the woman occupies a relatively important

place, especially·in that of the Hittites. But in none of them do we find that regard for the slave which is so prominent a feature in the religious teaching of ancient Egypt. The slave was a chattel and nothing else. Those who wish to study the Code of the Hittites can now do so in the translation of it by that pioneer of Hittite decipherment, Professor Hrozny (*Code Hittite*, Paris, 1922).

APPENDIX

I.—EXTRACTS RELATING TO THE HITTITES FROM THE TEL EL-AMARNA LETTERS.

FROM a letter of Dusratta, king of Mitanni : " When all the [army] of the Hittites marched to attack my country, Tessub my lord gave it into my hands and I smote it. There was none among them who returned to his own land."

From a letter of Aziru, son of Ebed-Asherah the Amorite, to the Egyptian official Dûdu : " O my lord now Khatip (Hotep) is with me. I and he will come (together). O my lord, the king of the land of the Hittites has marched into the land of Nukhassi (*Egyptian* Anaugas), and I am not strong enough to move, but let the king of the Hittites depart and then I and Khatip will come."

From a letter of Aziru to the Egyptian official Khai : " The king of the land of the Hittites is in Nukhassi, and I am afraid of him ; I keep guard lest he make his way up into the land of the Amorites. And if the city of Tunip falls there will be two roads (open) to the place where he is, and I am afraid of him, and on this account I have remained (here) till his departure. But now I and Khatip will march at once."

From a letter of Aziru to the Pharaoh : " And now the king of the Hittites is in Nukhassi : there are two roads to Tunip, and I am afraid it will fall, and that the city [will not be strong enough] to defend itself."

From a letter of Akizzi, the governor of Qatna (in Nukhassi) on the Khabur to the Pharaoh : " O my lord, the Sun-god my father made thy fathers and set his name upon them ; but now the king of the Hittites has taken the Sun-god my father, and my lord knows what are the acts of the gods, how they stand. And now the Sun-god my father will return to me, and the heart of my lord knows it, and let him give gold in plenty to the Sun-god my father as they (thy fathers) did. And my lord will receive a name from the Sun-god as in former days."

From another letter of Akizzi to Amon-hotep III : " And now [the king my lord] has sent to me asking [what] relations I have had with the king of the Hittites. [And to this] I reply, If I [receive anything from] the king of the Hittites I will send it to Egypt to the king my lord· . . . O my lord, Teuwatti of the city of Lapana and Arzauya of the city of Rukhizi are in league with Aidag-gama and the land of [Hobah ? and] the country of my lord is burned with fire. O my lord, even as I love the king my lord, so also do the kings of Nukhassi, of Ni, of Zinzar, and of Tunanat, for all these kings are servants of my lord. . . . O my lord, if Arzauya of Rukhizi and Teu-watti of Lapana are in the land of Ubi (Biblical Hobah) and Dasa is in the land of Amma, then my lord knows of them that the land of Ubi is lost to my lord. Daily do they send to Aidaggama (saying) : go and seize all the land of Ubi."

From a letter of Rib-Hadad, the Governor of Gebal : " And now again the soldiers of the lands of the Hittites are carrying away the governors of Gebal; so give counsel to Gebal."

From a letter of Ili-rabikh of Gebal : " Behold, Aziru (the Amorite) has killed Aduna king of Arqa. He has also killed the king of Ammiya (on the banks of the Euphrates and Sajur), and the king of Arvad and the (Egyptian) commissioner, and has taken their cities for himself. Simyra (Zemar) too, is his ; (yet they are all) cities of the king. Gebal alone is left to the king. Moreover, behold, Simyra and Ullazza have been taken by storm. Moreover, behold, Aziru . . . (has intrigued with) Itakama [and] has smitten all the lands of Amki, even the lands of the king. And now he has sent his men to occupy the lands of Amki and (other) places. Further, no action has been taken on the part of the king of the Hittites and the king of Narima (Naharaim) and [the king of Babylonia]."

From a letter of Batti-il (Bethuel) and another official to the king : " Moreover Hittite soldiers have captured Lupakku : the cities of the land of Amki and then the cities of Ben-Hadad have they also taken."

From a letter of Bêri of Khasabu : " Behold, we were acting for the land of Amki (and) the cities of the king my lord when Edagama of the city of Kinza came [at] the head of the soldiers of the Hittites."

From a letter of El-daia[n] of Khazi (near Shechem) : " Behold, we were acting for the land of Amki (and) the cities of the king my lord when Edagama of Kinza came at the head of the soldiers of the Hittites [to seize the cities of the king my lord]."

From Abimelech the governor of Tyre : " The king

my lord sent to me saying, What thou hearest about the land of Canaan write to me. (Know then that) the king of the land of Danuna (the Danaans ?) is dead and his brother reigns in his stead, and his country is tranquil. And the king must learn (?) that the city of Ugarit (on the northern coast of Syria) has been consumed by fire ; half of it is consumed, and the other half, where is it ? And the soldiers of the Hittites, where are they ? Etagama the lord of Kadesh and Aziru have made war against Namyawaza " (the governor of Kumidi near Kadesh).

II.—LIST OF HITTITE KINGS.

	B.C.
Pamba, antagonist of Naram-Sin	cir. 2700
Biyustis	2300
Dudkhaliyas I, Tid'al in Gen. xiv.	2050
Labarnas, and queen Tawanunas	1900
Mursilis I, son, captured Babylon	1875
Bimbiras	—
Khantelis	—
Bisenis	—
Zidantas, and queen Iyayas	—
Ammunas	—
Zurus	—
Titiyas	—
Khuzziyas, and queen Summuris	—

	B.C.
Telibinus I, captured Damascus . . .	1700
Mursilis II	—

Dudkhaliyas II	1430
Khattusilis II	—
Subbi-luliuma, his son	1400
Letter to Akhenaten of Egypt	1383
Arnuwandas I, his son	—
Mursilis III, his brother	1350
Muwatallis or Mutallis, his son	—
War with Ramses II of Egypt	1292
Urkhi-Tessub, his son	—
Khattusilis III, his uncle, treaty with Egypt .	1280
Dudkhaliyas III, his son	—
Arnuwandas II, his son	—
Dudkhaliyas IV, his son	—
Fall of the First Hittite Empire	1200
Rise of the Moscho-Hittite power at Tyana. .	1200
Carchemish captured by the Assyrians . .	717

INDEX

LIST OF SCRIPTURE REFERENCES